Oxford Reading Tree
SONG BOOK AND CD

JAN HOLDSTOCK

Illustrations by Alex Brychta and Jan Brychta
based on Oxford Reading Tree stories by Roderick Hunt

(for Key Stage 1)

Music Department

Oxford University Press

Oxford New York

Music Department, Oxford University Press,
Great Clarendon Street, Oxford OX2 6DP

Oxford   New York
Athens   Auckland   Bangkok   Bogotá   Buenos Aires   Calcutta
Cape Town   Chennai   Dar es Salaam   Delhi   Florence   Hong Kong   Istanbul
Karachi   Kuala Lumpur   Madrid   Melbourne   Mexico City   Mumbai
Nairobi   Paris   São Paulo   Singapore   Taipei   Tokyo   Toronto   Warsaw

and associated companies in
Berlin   Ibadan

Oxford is a trade mark of Oxford University Press

© Oxford University Press 1998

The moral rights of the author have been asserted.

All rights reserved. With the exception of the piano accompaniment pages, which may be reproduced for non-commercial use within the classroom, no part of this publication may be reproduced, stored in a retrieval system, or transmitted, in any form or by any means, except in accordance with the terms of licences issued by the Copyright Licensing Agency, or except for fair dealing for the purpose of research or private study, or criticism or review, as permitted under the Copyright, Designs and Patents Act, 1988. Enquiries concerning reproduction outside those terms should be addressed to the Music Department, Oxford University Press.

Permission to perform the work in public should normally be obtained from the Performing Right Society Ltd., (PRS), 29/33 Berners Street, London W1P 4AA, or its affiliated Societies in each country throughout the world, unless the owner or the occupier of the premises being used holds a licence from the Society.

Permission to make a recording must be obtained in advance from the Mechanical Copyright Protection Society Ltd., (MCPS), Elgar House, 41 Streatham High Road, London SW16 1ER, or its affiliated Societies in each country throughout the world.

The purchaser of the book and CD may make a single cassette copy of part or all of the CD for educational purposes only. Multiple copies may not be made, and no copies may be sold.

The piano accompaniment pages may be photocopied for ease of use, by the purchaser only.

ISBN 0–19–321369–9

10 9 8 7 6 5 4 3 2 1

Acknowledgement
Cover illustration by Alex Brychta

Typeset by Barnes Music Engraving Ltd., E. Sussex.
Printed and bound in Great Britain.

Contents

	Page	CD track
Foreword by Roderick Hunt	4	
Preface by Jan Holdstock	4	
Note to Teachers	5	
Kipper's Here at the Nursery	6	1
Something To Do Today	7	2
Stop and Go	8	3
The Haircut	9	4
The Lost Teddy	10	5
The Library	11	6
The Swing Ball	12	7
Painted Faces	13	
Let's Have a House	14	
See if Floppy Knows	15	
Frightening Sounds	16	
The Apple	17	
The Toys' Party	18	8
New Trainers	19	9
A New Dog	20	10
What a Bad Dog!	21	11
Let's Take Turns	22	12
The Dreadful Dragon	23	13
Hoppy's Bath	24	14
The Baby-sitter	25	15
The Water Fight	26	16
Kipper's Balloon	27	17
Spots!	28	18
It's Party Time	29	19

	Page	CD track
Kipper's Laces	30	20
Tooth Fairy	31	21
The Foggy Day	32	22
Biff's Aeroplane	33	23
Floppy the Hero	34	24
Mum Never Knew	35	25
The Headache	36	26
At the Park	37	27
Fancy Dress	38	28
Push!	39	29
Good Old Mum	40	30
The Pet Shop	41	31
Everyone's Doing It	42	32
Making Faces	43	33
The Journey	44	34
It's No Fun!	45	35
We're All Telling Tales	46	36
Sugar Calypso	47	37
At the Zoo	48	38
Hey Presto!	49	39
It's the Weather	50	40
The Orange Duck	51	41
A Safe Place	52	42
Creepy-crawly	53	43
Guitar Chords	54	
Piano Accompaniments	56	

Foreword

What could be a more enjoyable and meaningful way to share reading than by singing songs based on the Oxford Reading Tree stories and characters? And with 48 songs and activities, this song book is a real treasure trove of material.

Jan Holdstock has achieved a notable success – a song book and CD that can be used simply and to such great effect by *all* teachers, whether or not they have specialist knowledge of music. Children will immediately respond to these lively and catchy songs, which they will find easy to learn, and great fun to sing.

I thoroughly recommend this material. The songs have been skilfully written to incorporate much of the language of the original stories and to reflect their humour. The wide variety of activities that accompany the songs are a terrific bonus.

The Oxford Reading Tree song book is a resource that no teacher or school should be without. And as a way of teaching a wide range of reading skills to a large group of children while having tremendous fun at the same time – well, it is unbeatable!

Roderick Hunt

Preface

I have greatly enjoyed writing these songs and activities to support the first few stories in the Oxford Reading Tree. Meeting Kipper, Biff, Chip, and all the other Reading Tree characters was a delight, and the combination of Roderick's stories and Alex's pictures was just right to set the poems and tunes going through my head.

The songs are all simple and catchy, whether they use well-known tunes or new ones, and I've used lots of different styles. The CD is exciting too, using all sorts of rhythms and instrumental sounds to accompany the singers.

Some of the songs, like 'The Toys' Party', follow the story through the book page by page. Others, like the 'Tooth Fairy', give the children a chance to bring their own experience to one aspect of the story. Cumulative songs like 'The Baby-sitter' give extra practice in sequencing the events of a story – use the pictures in the book to stop you getting lost in these.

'Let's Take Turns' and 'A Safe Place' would be useful songs for assembly, while game songs like 'Stop and Go' or 'Kipper's Balloon' are more suited to the classroom. But whatever you do with the songs in the book or on the CD, I hope you all have lots of fun with them.

Jan Holdstock

Note to Teachers

Accompaniments

Where you see this icon on the page, you'll find a suggested percussion part. Small children find it easiest to add percussion to a song if they can either play on a definite word or play in a definite space. Where the instrument is played on a word, the word is **bold**; where the instrument fills a gap you will see a note like this:

Provide small light instruments which the children can play comfortably, then discuss with the class which sound would suit the words of the song. Tell each child which is 'their' word or 'their' space – you can share the words round if you like.

Your players will need lots of help to keep in time. Encourage them to watch you really carefully and play with you when you play, clap, or point. Whatever they are playing, don't let them make too big a movement – taking a wild swing at a drum will make the sound late. When the instrument is not being played, put it down carefully on the carpet or on a carpet square.

Where you see this icon I've written a piano accompaniment, which you'll find at the back of the book.

Chord symbols are added to the songs, and guitar players will find useful information (charts and capo suggestions) on pages 54–5.

The CD

Information about the verses and choruses included on the CD is given in the top right-hand corner of each song page, together with the track number, which is also included on the contents page. The accompaniments and singing are tracked separately on the CD, so, if you wish, you can turn the volume off one track to play just the accompaniment. For convenience, the CD may be copied to cassette.

Singing

Singing requires concentration, and it is easy for the children to switch off. Their mouths may be moving, but their eyes tell you that their minds are elsewhere! Today's children are better 'lookers' than 'listeners', so when you engage their eyes as well as their ears it helps to focus their attention.

If you are singing with the CD, listen to it first and discuss it with the children, showing them the pictures in the reading book as you do so. While it is important to hold the children's attention, don't press them to join in. Keep reminding them to use their *singing* voices, as even those who sing really well forget when the song is new to them.

Ask the children whether the singers sound jolly or sad or fierce or thoughtful. Encourage the children to show these feelings in their own singing. If you are singing with the children, encourage them to look at your face, as you can help them with your own expression; and if you breathe in before each phrase, some of them will copy you. Why not invite a few children to the front and ask the class to sing to them: this will focus the class singing and keep their attention from drifting away. The children at the front could help by doing an appropriate action for each verse.

Enjoy singing these songs!

Jan Holdstock

Stage 1 Kipper stories: At School

CD track 1: Two verses and choruses

Kipper's Here at the Nursery

𝅗𝅥 = 76

CHORUS

Kip-per's here at the nur-sery, he did-n't want to come to-day. There are so ma-ny things to play with, he does-n't want to go a-way. **End here**

VERSE

1. Let's do some cook-ing, **that's fun to do.** Let's do some build-ing, **we'll do it too.** Let's do some cook-ing, **that's fun to do.** Let's do some build-ing, **we'll do it too.** **Repeat Chorus**

Suggestions for extra verses.

2. Let's play at houses, that's fun to do. } repeat
   Let's play with this car, we'll do it too.
   CHORUS: Kipper's here at the nursery ...

3. Let's do some cleaning, that's fun to do. } repeat
   Let's do some ironing, we'll do it too.

4. Let's play with teddy, that's fun to do. } repeat
   Let's play with water, we'll do it too.

5. Let's eat our dinner, that's fun to do. } repeat
   Let's eat an apple, we'll do it too.

Play the rhythm of the words in **this type.**

6

Stage 1 Kipper stories: Getting Up

CD track 2: *All verses*

Something To Do Today

♩ = 72

CHORUS

Hur - ry, hur - ry! Get - ting all rea - dy! Some - thing to do to - day!

Hur - ry, hur - ry! Get - ting all rea - dy! Some - thing to do to - day!

End here

VERSE

1. It's my dad's birth - day, ✗ let's make a ban - ner.* ✗

Verse — to Chorus — **Repeat Chorus**

Verse 1 fits pages 1 to 7; verses 2 to 4 fit the last page.

For verses 2 to 4, at * add an extra line for each verse, repeating the music of the *italic* section.

2. It's my dad's birthday, let's make a banner.
   Let's wrap his presents, let's find some paper.
   CHORUS: Hurry, hurry! . . .

3. It's my dad's birthday, let's make a banner.
   Let's wrap his presents, let's find some paper.
   Let's wave a rattle, let's bang a tin tray.
   CHORUS: Hurry, hurry! . . .

4. It's my dad's birthday, let's make a banner.
   Let's wrap his presents, let's find some paper.
   Let's wave a rattle, let's bang a tin tray.
   Let's play the trumpet. 'Woof-woof' goes Floppy.
   CHORUS: Hurry, hurry! . . .

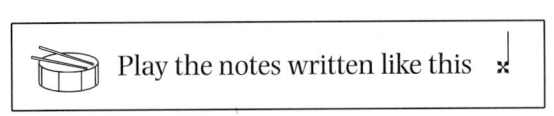

Play the notes written like this ✗

Stage 1 Kipper stories: Look Out! CD track 3: *Twice through*

Stop and Go

Tune: In a cottage in a wood

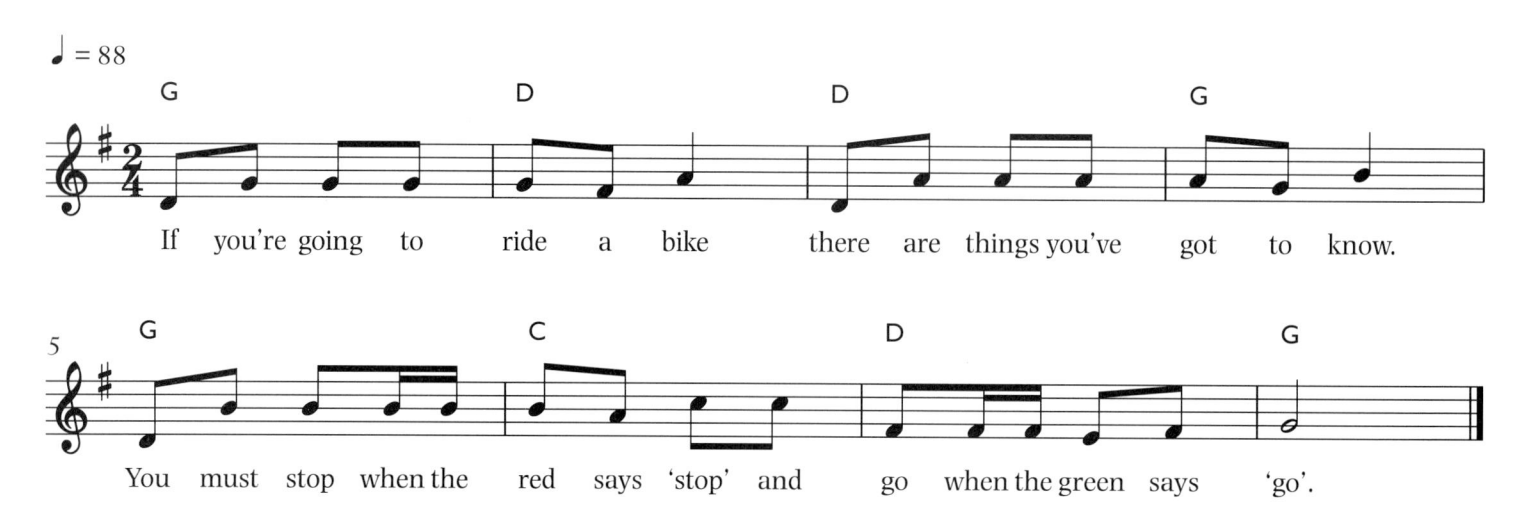

♩ = 88

If you're going to ride a bike there are things you've got to know.
You must stop when the red says 'stop' and go when the green says 'go'.

For this activity you will need a card with a red circle (stop) on one side and a green circle (go) on the other.

When the children know the song, explain to them that while you are holding up the green circle they must sing the song. When you are holding up the red circle they must not sing, but they must 'think' the song in their heads. When you hold up the green circle again, is everyone in the same place in the music?

8

The Haircut

Verse 1 fits pages 1 to 3.

2. *(pages 4 and 5)*
   They're going to wash our hair now, splash splash!
   They're going to wash our hair now, splash splash!
   They'll wash you and me too with shampoo.
   They're going to wash our hair now, splash splash!

3. *(pages 6 and 7)*
   They're going to use the scissors, look now!
   They're going to use the scissors, look now!
   They snip snip and clip clip, quick, quick, quick!
   They're going to use the scissors, look now!

4. *(last page)*
   We're showing it to Mum now, oh no!
   We're showing it to Mum now, oh no!
   It looks wrong! It's all gone! I liked it long!
   We're showing it to Mum now, oh no!

Stage 1 Kipper stories: The Lost Teddy CD track 5: Verses 1, 2, 5, and 6

The Lost Teddy

Tune: Follow me to London

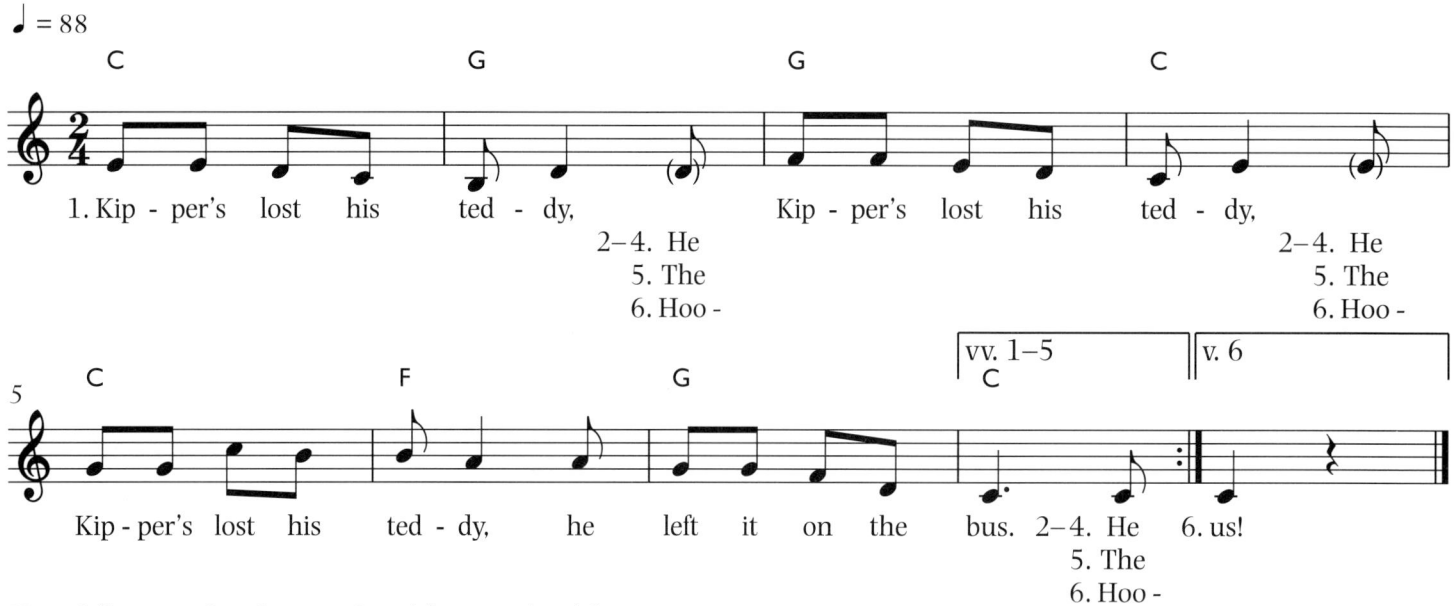

♩ = 88

1. Kip-per's lost his ted-dy, Kip-per's lost his ted-dy, Kip-per's lost his ted-dy, he left it on the bus.
   2–4. He / 5. The / 6. Hoo-

Verse 1 fits pages 1 to 3; verses 2 to 4 fit pages 4 and 5.

2. He doesn't want a soldier,
   he doesn't want a soldier,
   he only wants his teddy,
   he left it on the bus.

3. He doesn't want a toy dog,
   he doesn't want a toy dog,
   he only wants his teddy,
   he left it on the bus.

4. He doesn't want a toy cat,
   he doesn't want a toy cat,
   he only wants his teddy,
   he left it on the bus.

5. (*pages 6 and 7*)
   The lady in the office,
   the lady in the office,
   will look for Kipper's teddy,
   he left it on the bus.

6. (*page 8*)
   Hooray! He's found his teddy!
   Hooray! He's found his teddy!
   Hooray! He's found his teddy!
   Let's take him home with us!

Stage 1 Kipper stories: The Library   CD track 6: One verse

The Library

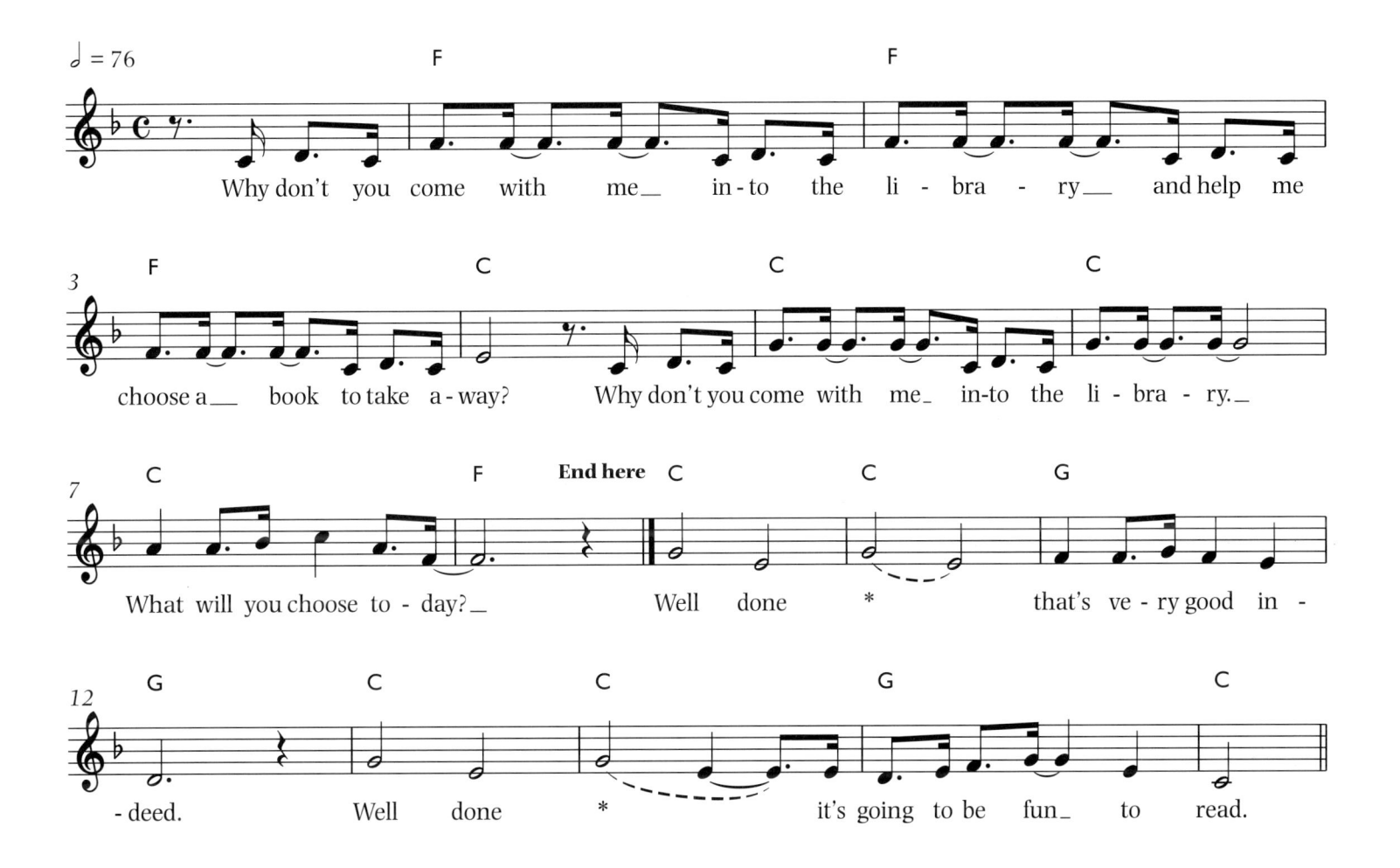

♩ = 76

Why don't you come with me — in-to the li - bra - ry — and help me choose a — book to take a - way? Why don't you come with me — in-to the li - bra - ry. — What will you choose to - day? — Well done * that's ve - ry good in - deed. Well done * it's going to be fun — to read.

- Get out a selection of library books and put them where the children can see them.

- Choose a child (Kipper) to stand with you at the front of the class.

- *After 'What will you choose today?' Kipper chooses one of the books. Then everyone sings 'Well done, Kipper' etc.

- Kipper can also have a chance to say why he's chosen the book.

- Choose another child (e.g. Biff) and repeat the activity.

The Swing Ball

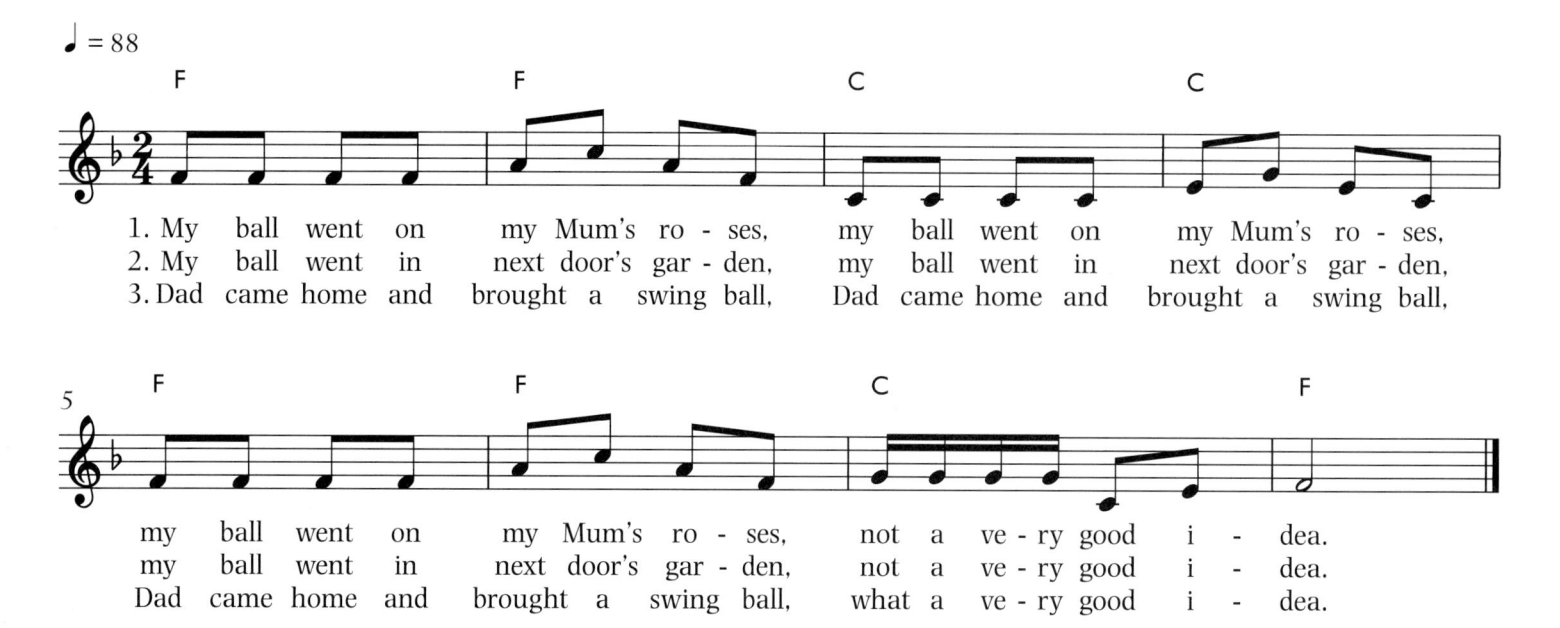

♩ = 88

1. My ball went on my Mum's ro - ses, my ball went on my Mum's ro - ses,
2. My ball went in next door's gar - den, my ball went in next door's gar - den,
3. Dad came home and brought a swing ball, Dad came home and brought a swing ball,

my ball went on my Mum's ro - ses, not a ve - ry good i - dea.
my ball went in next door's gar - den, not a ve - ry good i - dea.
Dad came home and brought a swing ball, what a ve - ry good i - dea.

Verse 1 fits page 1; verse 2 pages 4 and 5; verse 3 pages 6 to 8.

Other suitable verses would be:

My ball went and hit my brother,
my ball went and hit my brother,
my ball went and hit my brother,
not a very good idea.

My ball went and broke the window . . . etc.

Stage 1 Biff and Chip stories: The Street Fair — *No recording*

Painted Faces

> Eight clean faces
> standing in the queue.
> One gets painted,
> seven more to do.

For this activity you will need to make eight flash cards. Each should have a 'clean' face on one side and a painted face on the other. The children will enjoy doing this.

- Eight children stand in a line holding the flash cards with the clean faces showing.

- Point along the line while the class says steadily:
  clean face, clean face, clean face, clean face, clean face, clean face, clean face, clean face.

- Everybody says the poem.

- Choose a child who is not standing in the line to turn over one of the cards. Now you might get:
  clean face, clean face, clean face, clean face, painted face, clean face, clean face, clean face.

- Carry on until all the cards are all showing 'painted face'.

Stage 1   Biff and Chip stories: The Big Box

Let's Have a House

Let's have a house!
Oh yes!
Let's have a door!
Oh yes!
Let's have windows!
Oh yes!
Let's have a floor!
Oh yes!

The rain came down!
Oh no!
It rained on the door!
Oh no!
It rained through the windows!
Oh no!
It rained on the floor!
Oh no!

For this activity you will need to provide a selection of instruments.

- Read the poem to the children.

- Ask the children to join in with 'oh yes' and 'oh no'.

- Try using one or two instruments to play along with 'oh yes' and 'oh no'. Make sure that the players play two sounds.

- Divide into two groups. One group says the poem and the other says 'oh yes' and 'oh no'.

Stage 1 Biff and Chip stories: Fetch! *No recording*

See if Floppy Knows

The drum's in the circle,
round and round it goes.
Who's going to play it?
See if Floppy knows.

For this activity you will need a drum and a 'Floppy' hat, mask or blindfold, to cover one child's eyes.

- The children sit in a circle.

- One child is chosen to be Floppy, and stands in the circle, wearing the 'Floppy' hat.

- A drum is passed round the circle, while everyone says the poem.

- When the poem stops, the child holding the drum plays it and Floppy tries to find it.

Other instruments can be substituted, for a change.

Stage 1 Biff and Chip stories: The Hedgehog — No recording

Frightening Sounds

Hedgehog, hedgehog,
trot around,
till you hear a frightening sound.
Then its time to curl up small
like a little ball.

For this activity you will need to provide a selection of instruments or noise-makers.

- Read the poem to the children.

- Ask the children to practise curling up as small as they can.

- Discuss the fact that very quiet sounds are sometimes the most frightening.

- Choose one child to make a frightening sound.

- Use voice sounds, body sounds, or instruments.

- Invite the children to trot round while you all say the poem. At the end of it, the chosen child makes the frightening sound and everybody curls up.

The Apple

Can you see?
High up in the apple tree,
one red apple,
it must be for me.

You will need a drum for this activity.

- Read the poem to the children.

- Ask the children to make up an action for each line and perform the actions while you read the poem.

- Tap the **rhythm** of the poem on a drum while the children perform the actions.

- Mix up the lines of the poem and see if the children can make the appropriate actions.

- Now let a child be the drummer.

Stage 2 Trunk stories: The Toys' Party CD track 8: Verses 1 to 4

The Toys' Party

Tune: Okey kokey

♩ = 120

1. You get a great big spoon, you get the big bowl out, *you put the corn flakes in and stir them all about.* We're going to have a par-ty and we need a cake, that's what it's all a-bout. Oh squid-gy squid-gy squid-gy, oh slop-py slop-py slop-py, oh stick-y stick-y stick-y, that's what it's all a-bout.

Verse 1 fits page 8.

For further verses, replace the words in *italics* with:

2. *. . . you put the sauce right in and stir it all about.* (*page 9*)

3. *. . . you put the milk right in and stir it all about.* (*page 10*)

4. *. . . you put the jam right in and stir it all about.* (*page 11*)

5. *. . . you put the sugar in and stir it all about.* (*page 12*)

6. *. . . you put the baked beans in and stir them all about.* (*page 13*)

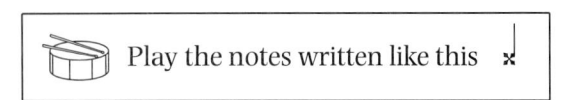

Play the notes written like this ✗

18

Stage 2 Trunk stories: New Trainers   CD track 9: All verses

New Trainers

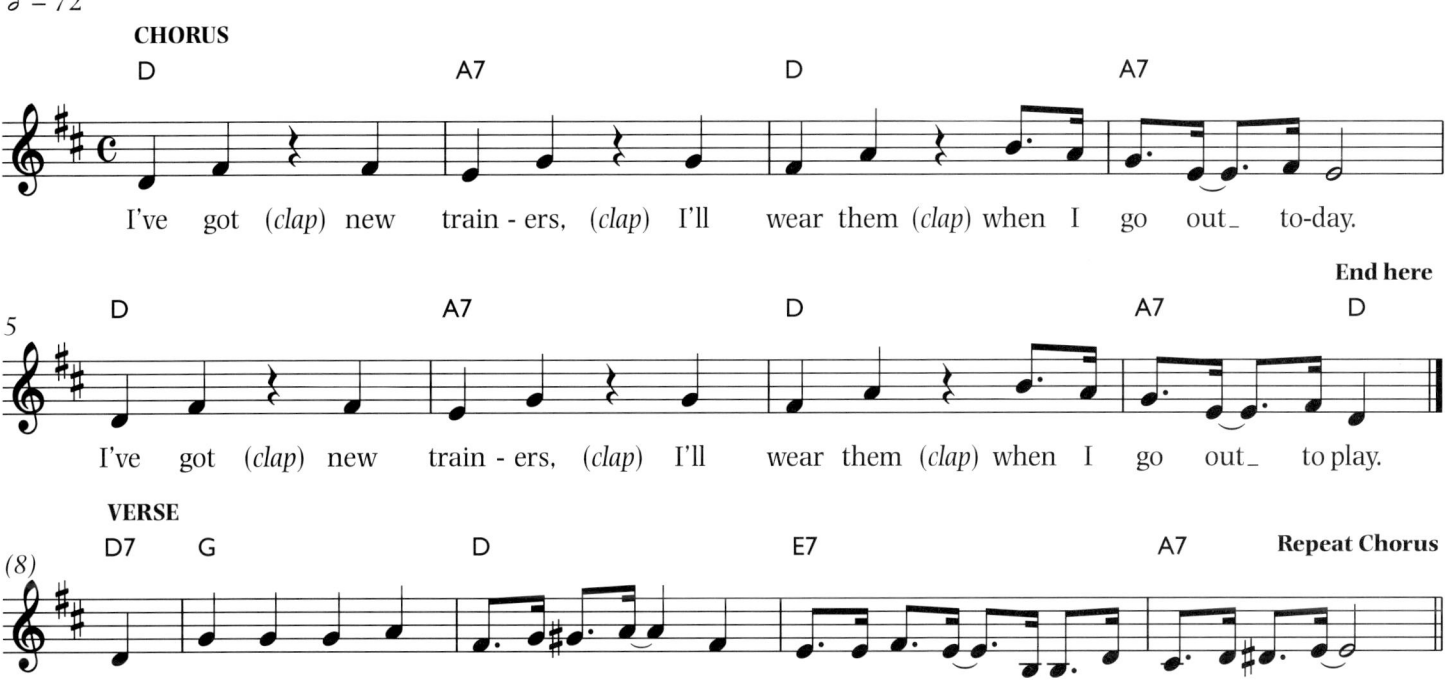

♩ = 72

CHORUS

I've got (clap) new train-ers, (clap) I'll wear them (clap) when I go out to-day.

I've got (clap) new train-ers, (clap) I'll wear them (clap) when I go out to play. **End here**

VERSE — **Repeat Chorus**

1. There's just one thing I must-n't for-get, they must-n't get dir-ty, they must-n't get wet.

Verse 1 fits page 4.

2. (*page 8*)
   Now I've been playing footie today,
   my trainers are dirty, all muddy and grey.
   CHORUS: I've got . . .

3. (*page 10*)
   I tried to walk on slippery rocks,
   my trainers are soggy and so are my socks.
   CHORUS: I've got . . .

4. (*page 14*)
   I've washed them now, they're lovely and clean.
   But now it's my Dad's turn – just look where he's been!
   CHORUS: I've got . . .

Page 56

19

Stage 2 Trunk stories: A New Dog

CD track 10: *All verses*

A New Dog

Tune: Did you ever see a lassie

1. Oh we've got to choose the right dog, the right dog, the right dog. Oh we've got to choose the right dog to take home to-day. We'll **feed** it and **brush** it and **walk** it and **love** it, So we've got to choose the right dog to take home to-day.

Verse 1 fits page 2; the following verses fit pages 8 to 15.

2. Oh why can't we have a big dog, a big dog, a big dog?
   Oh why can't we have a big dog to take home today?
   A **big** dog might **scare** you, might **scare** you, might **scare** you,
   And we've got to choose the right dog to take home today.

3. Oh why can't we have a little dog, a little dog, a little dog?
   Oh why can't we have a little dog to take home today?
   A **little** dog might **trip** you, might **trip** you, might **trip** you,
   And we've got to have the right dog to take home today.

4. Oh why can't we have a strong dog, a strong dog, a strong dog?
   Oh why can't we have a strong dog to take home today?
   A **strong** dog might **pull** you, might **pull** you, might **pull** you,
   And we've got to have the right dog to take home today.

5. Oh yes, everyone likes this dog, likes this dog, likes this dog.
   Oh yes, everyone likes this dog, we'll have him today.
   He's gentle and soppy, so we'll call him Floppy.
   Oh yes, everyone likes this dog, we'll have him today.

> Play the rhythm of the words in **this type.**

** For capo chords see page 55.

Stage 2 Trunk stories: What a Bad Dog! CD track 11: *All verses*

What a Bad Dog!

Tune: Ten green bottles

♩ = 100

1–4. You're a **bad dog**, Flop-py, we're ve-ry cross with you.
5. You're a **good dog**, Flop-py, we're ve-ry pleased with you.

Bad dog, Flop-py, we're ve-ry cross with you. You *went on the con-crete*, what a
Good dog, Flop-py, we're ve-ry pleased with you. You *saved the house from burn-ing*, what a

naugh-ty thing to do. You're a **bad dog**, Flop-py, we're ve-ry cross with you!
cle-ver thing to do. You're a **good dog**, Flop-py, we're ve-ry pleased with you!

Verse 1 fits page 1.

For the following verses, replace the words in *italics* with:

2. *You got all muddy, . . .* (page 2)

3. *You pulled down the washing, . . .* (page 4)

4. *You pushed the Lego over, . . .* (page 6)

5. (page 16)

> 🥁 Play the rhythm of the words in **this type**.

21

Stage 2 Trunk stories: The Go-kart
CD track 12: Twice through

Let's Take Turns

Echo song

♩ = 120

Let's take turns, (let's take turns). Me and you, (me and you).
Let's take turns, (let's take turns). E-very-thing we do, (e-very-thing we do).
Play-ing a game, (play-ing a game). Hav-ing a ride, (hav-ing a ride).
We'll have fun, (we'll have fun). Side by side, (side by side). Let's take turns,
(let's take turns). E-very-day, (e-very-day). Let's take turns, (let's take turns).
E-very time we play, (e-very time we play). Let's take turns, (let's take turns). Then join to-ge-ther to
say, 'We're going to have fun be-cause we know the way'.

Page 57

Stage 2 Trunk stories: The Dream CD track 13: All verses

The Dreadful Dragon

♩ = 136

1. There once was a dreadful dragon, it came to Biff one night *with terrible teeth and cruel claws it was looking for a fight. Poor old Biff, what a horrible dream, it gave you a nasty fright. Give yourself a shake! Now you're wide awake! Everything's quite all right.

*Make further verses by replacing the words in *italics* with:

2. ... *with evil eyes and a twisted tail* ...

3. ... *with wicked wings and spiky scales* ...

Play the notes written like this ✗

Page 56

23

Stage 2 More stories A: Floppy's Bath CD track 14: Verses 1 to 4

Floppy's Bath

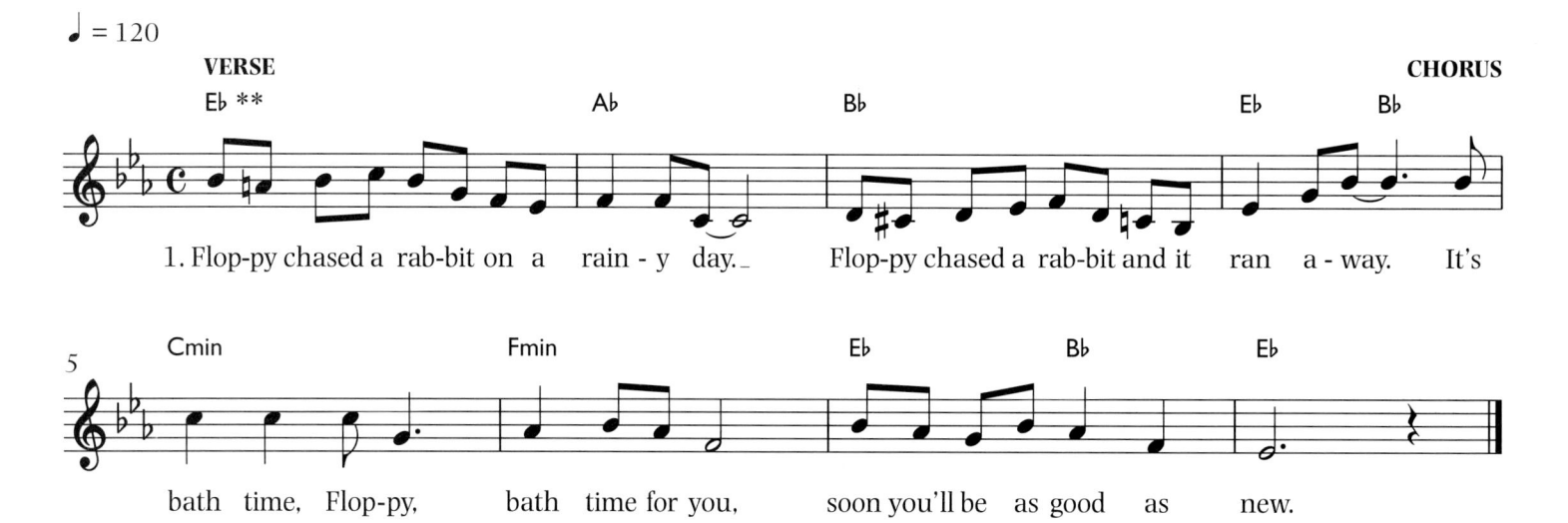

♩ = 120

1. Flop-py chased a rab-bit on a rain-y day. Flop-py chased a rab-bit and it ran a-way. It's bath time, Flop-py, bath time for you, soon you'll be as good as new.

Verse 1 fits pages 1 to 8.

2. (*page 9*)
   Floppy's coat is soggy and his paws are brown.
   He'll mess up the carpet if we put him down.
   CHORUS: It's bath time, Floppy, . . .

3. (*pages 10 and 11*)
   He's so wet and muddy we know what to do.
   Put him in a bath with special dog shampoo.
   CHORUS: It's bath time, Floppy, . . .

4. (*pages 12 and 13*)
   Blow him with a drier 'til he's nice and clean.
   Nobody will ever know just where he's been.
   CHORUS: It's bath time, Floppy, . . .

5. Repeat verse 1 . . . and so on

** For capo chords see page 55.

The Baby-sitter

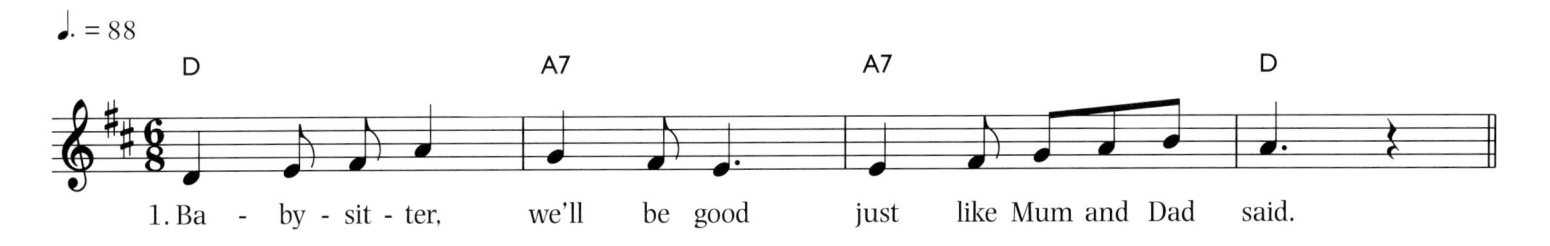

♩. = 88

1. Ba-by-sit-ter, we'll be good just like Mum and Dad said.
We'll just read a sto-ry* and then we'll go to bed.

For verses 2 to 6, at * add an extra line for each verse, repeating the music of the *italic* section.

2. We'll just read a story,
   we'll just watch the telly, (*page 6*)
   and then we'll go to bed.

3. We'll just read a story,
   we'll just watch the telly,
   we'll just play a record, (*page 6*)
   and then we'll go to bed.

4. ... *we'll just make a sandwich,* ... (*page 9*)

5. ... *we'll just make some cocoa,* ... (*page 9*)

6. ... *we'll just have a pillow fight,* ... (*page 10*)

(*The additional words for vv. 3 and 4 are excluded from the CD.)

Stage 2 More stories A: The Water Fight   CD track 16: Verses 1, 2, and 3

The Water Fight

Tune: Train is a-comin'

♩ = 152

1. Wa-ter in the hose-pipe, **swish swish.** Wa-ter in the hose-pipe, **swish swish.**
Wa-ter in the hose-pipe, wa-ter in the hose-pipe, wa-ter in the hose-pipe, **swish swish.**

Verse 1 fits page 4.

2. Water in the paddling pool, **splash splash.** (*page 4*)

3. Biff in the water, **oh no!** (*page 6*)

4. Water over Kipper, **oh no!** (*page 7*)

5. Floppy in the water, **woof woof!** (*page 8*)

6. Water over Mum, **'Stop it!'** (*page 10*)

7. Water in the bucket, **slop slop.** (*page 12*)

8. Water on the neighbour, **oh no!** (*page 15*)

Play the rhythm of the words in **this type.**

26

Stage 2 More stories A: Kipper's Balloon

CD track 17: Twice through

Kipper's Balloon

Tune: Row, row, row your boat

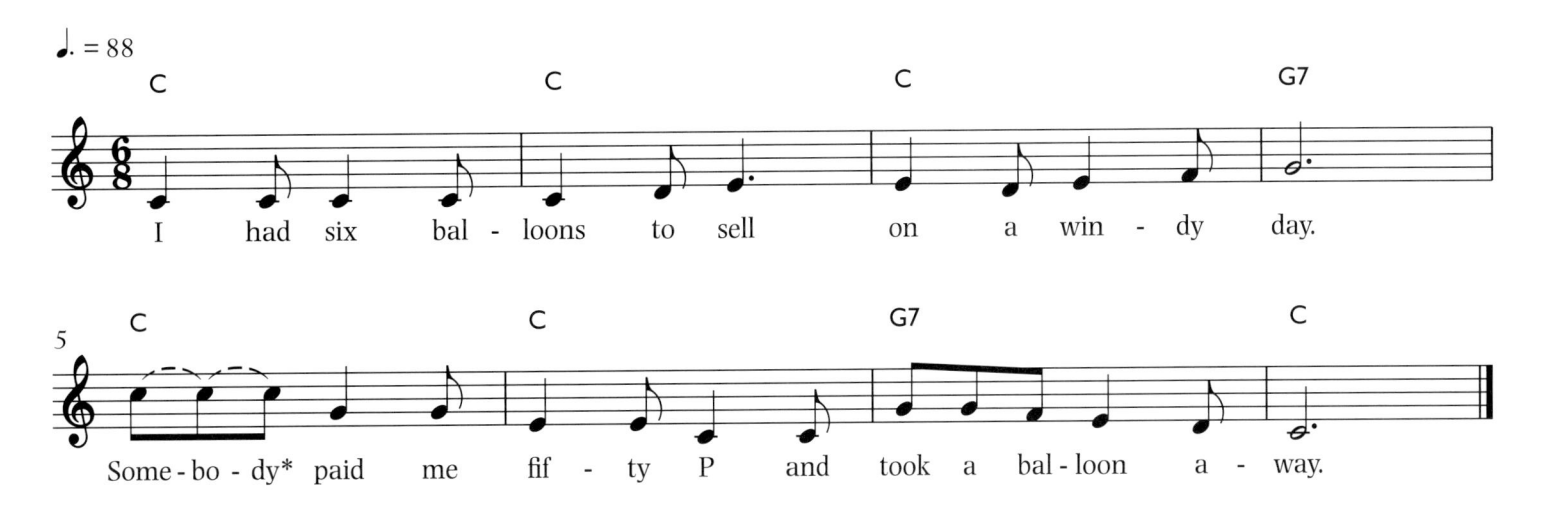

♩. = 88

I had six balloons to sell on a windy day.
Somebody* paid me fifty P and took a balloon away.

* Insert child's name.

For this activity you will need six balloons, or pictures of balloons.
You will also need a purse with six 50p pieces in it.

- The children sit in a circle and sing the song while the purse is passed round. At the end of the song the child with the purse 'buys' a balloon.

- The next verse starts 'I had five balloons to sell . . .'.

27

Stage 2 More stories A: Spots!

CD track 18: Verses 1, 2, 3, and 5

Spots!

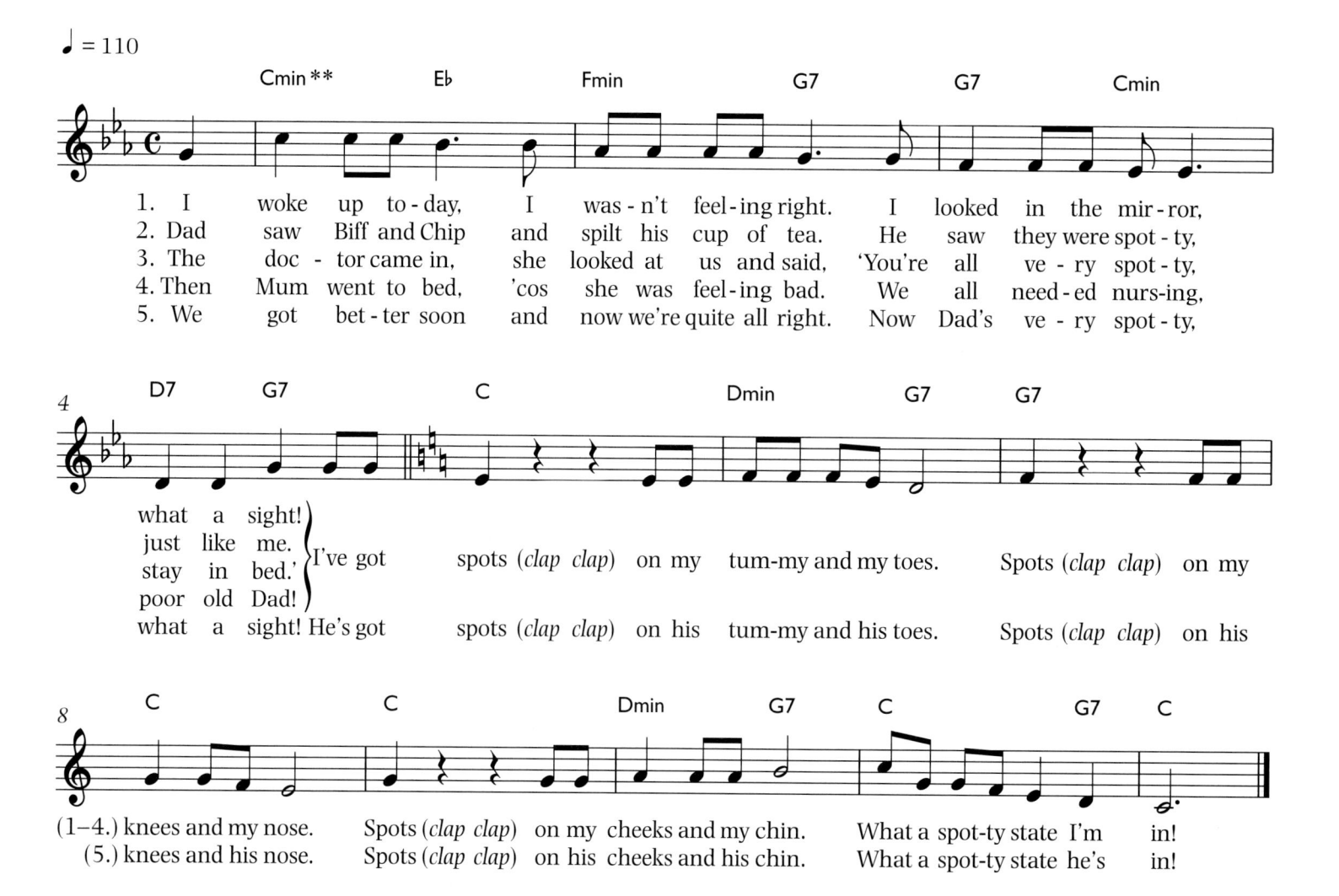

♩ = 110

1. I woke up to-day, I was-n't feel-ing right. I looked in the mir-ror,
2. Dad saw Biff and Chip and spilt his cup of tea. He saw they were spot-ty,
3. The doc-tor came in, she looked at us and said, 'You're all ve-ry spot-ty,
4. Then Mum went to bed, 'cos she was feel-ing bad. We all need-ed nurs-ing,
5. We got bet-ter soon and now we're quite all right. Now Dad's ve-ry spot-ty,

what a sight!
just like me. ⎫
stay in bed.' ⎬ I've got spots (*clap clap*) on my tum-my and my toes. Spots (*clap clap*) on my
poor old Dad! ⎭
what a sight! He's got spots (*clap clap*) on his tum-my and his toes. Spots (*clap clap*) on his

(1–4.) knees and my nose.   Spots (*clap clap*) on my cheeks and my chin.   What a spot-ty state I'm   in!
 (5.) knees and his nose.   Spots (*clap clap*) on his cheeks and his chin.   What a spot-ty state he's   in!

Verses 1 to 5 fit pages 1, 3, 4, 6, and 16.

Page 58

** For capo chords see page 55.

Stage 2 More stories A: Kipper's Birthday — CD track 19: Twice through

It's Party Time

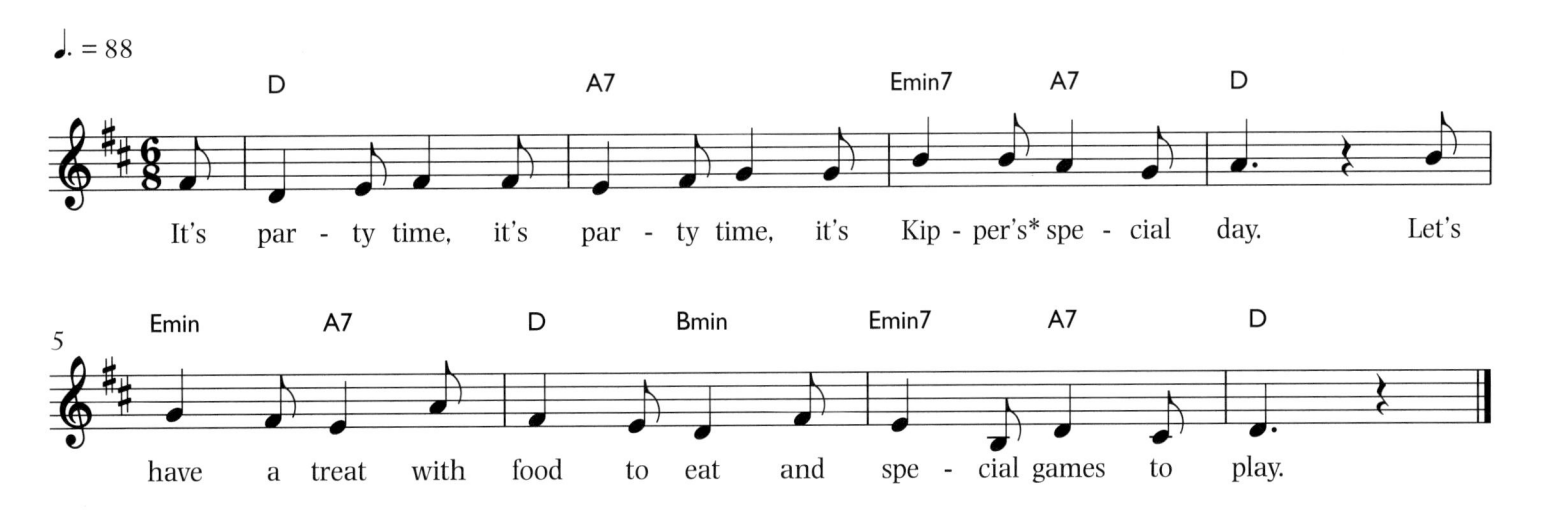

♩. = 88

It's par-ty time, it's par-ty time, it's Kip-per's* spe-cial day. Let's have a treat with food to eat and spe-cial games to play.

For this activity you will need a bubble-blowing kit.

- The children sit in a circle and pass a beanbag or small toy round while they sing the song. (At * use one of the children's names if appropriate.)

- When the song stops the child with the beanbag has a chance to blow a bubble.

- Ask the other children to watch the bubble and make a quiet sound with their voices (e.g. mmmm or shhhh) all the time they can see it. This is a useful and 'fun' way to practise the sounds of different letters.

Stage 2 More stories B: Kipper's Laces   CD track 20: Once through

Kipper's Laces

♩ = 120

Kip-per's la - ces went **wig-gle wig-gle wig-gle**. Kip-per's la - ces went **jig-gle jig-gle jig-gle**.

Kip-per's la - ces went **squig-gle squig-gle squig-gle**. Kip-per could-n't tie them yet.

Kip-per's la - ces went **wig-gle wig-gle wig-gle**. Kip-per's la - ces went **jig-gle jig-gle jig-gle**.

Kip-per's la - ces went **squig-gle squig-gle squig-gle**. Kip-per was up - set. So he

tried and tried, and tried and tried, and tried and tried all day. So he

tried and tried, and tried and tried, then he did it. Hoo - ray!

Play the rhythm of the words in **this type**.

Page 58

** For capo chords see page 55.

Stage 2 More stories B: The Wobbly Tooth
CD track 21: Twice through

Tooth Fairy

♩ = 72

Tooth fai - ry, where are you? I've got some-thing to say to you.

Tooth fai - ry, bring the mo - ney and take my tooth a - way.

*Twen - ty P, fif - ty P. How much will you pay?

Tooth fai - ry, bring the mo - ney and take my tooth a - way.

*The children will want to discuss how much the tooth fairy pays in their house. Insert their tooth prices at *.

Play the rhythm of the words in **this type**.

Page 59

Stage 2 More stories B: The Foggy Day   CD track 22: Verses 1, 5, and 6

The Foggy Day

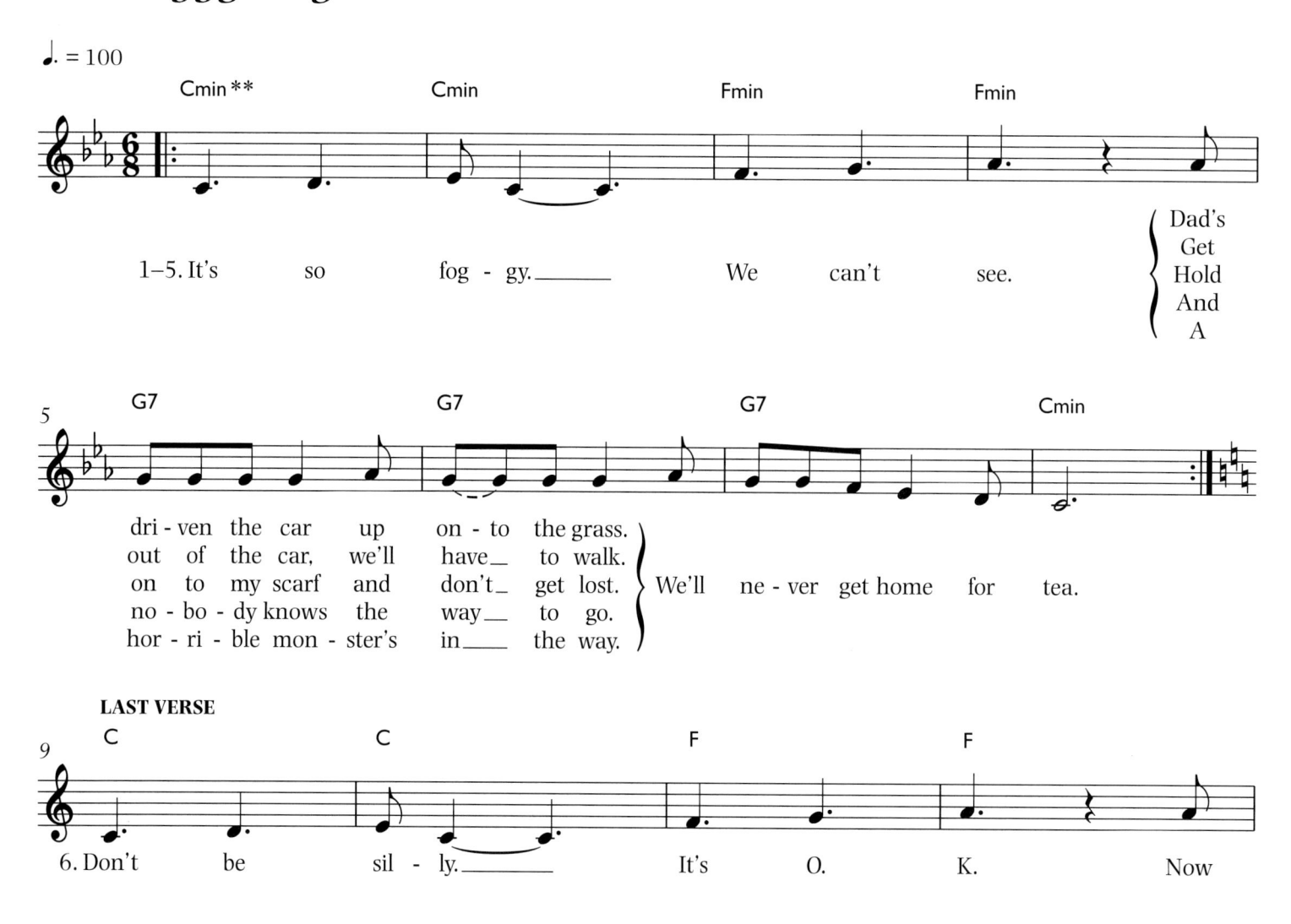

♩. = 100

1–5. It's so fog - gy. We can't see.
{ Dad's Get Hold And A }

dri - ven the car up on - to the grass.
out of the car, we'll have to walk.
on to my scarf and don't get lost. } We'll ne - ver get home for tea.
no - bo - dy knows the way to go.
hor - ri - ble mon - ster's in the way.

LAST VERSE

6. Don't be sil - ly. It's O. K. Now

Flop - py and Mum are say - ing 'Hel - lo'. We'll get our tea to - day.

Verses 1 to 5 fit pages 6, 8, 10, 12, and 14; verse 6 fits page 16.

Page 59

** For capo chords see page 55.

32

Biff's Aeroplane

Tune: Here we go round the mulberry bush

1. Biff made an **aeroplane**, aeroplane, aeroplane.
2. Biff flew the **aeroplane**, aeroplane, aeroplane.
3. Biff lost the **aeroplane**, aeroplane, aeroplane.

Biff made an **aeroplane**, painted white and red.
Biff flew the **aeroplane**, painted white and red.
Biff lost the **aeroplane**, painted white and red.

4. Everyone looked for the **aeroplane**, aeroplane, aeroplane.

Everyone looked for the **aeroplane**, painted white and red.

5. Biff found the **aeroplane**, aeroplane, aeroplane.

Biff found the **aeroplane**, she found it on her bed.

Verses 1 to 5 fit pages 1, 4, 8, 10, and 16.

Play the rhythm of the words in **this type**.

Stage 2 More stories B: Floppy the Hero CD track 24: All verses

Floppy the Hero

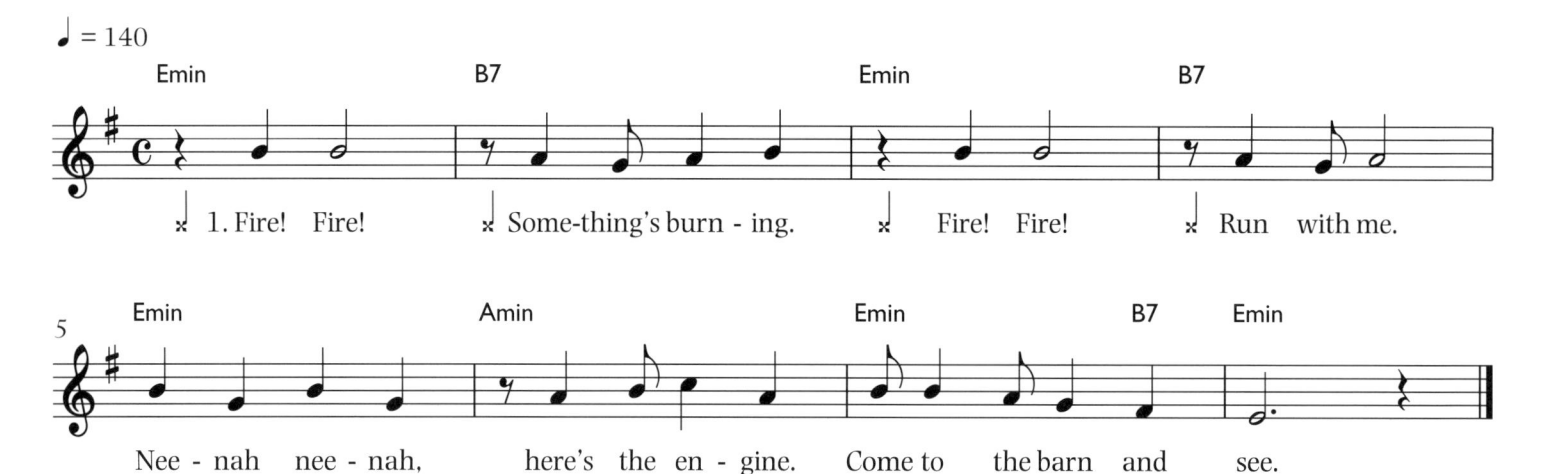

♩ = 140

1. Fire! Fire! Some-thing's burn-ing. Fire! Fire! Run with me.
Nee-nah nee-nah, here's the en-gine. Come to the barn and see.

Verse 1 fits pages 1 to 5.

2. (*pages 6 to 9*)
   Fire! Fire!
   Something's in there.
   Fire! Fire!
   Floppy knows.
   Woof woof woof woof,
   through the window.
   Into the barn he goes.

3. (*pages 10 to 13*)
   Fire! Fire!
   Push the door down.
   Fire! Fire!
   We can see.
   Squeak squeak squeak squeak,
   go the puppies.
   Floppy has set them free.

4. (*pages 14 to 16*)
   Floppy,
   you're a hero!
   Floppy,
   you're O.K.
   Bravo, bravo!
   Well done, Floppy.
   You're a good dog today.

Play the notes written like this ✗

Page 60

34

Stage 2 More stories B: The Chase CD track 25: *All verses*

Mum Never Knew

♩. = 88

(Verse, mm. 1–4): 1–4. Oh dear! Flop-py, what a naugh-ty thing to do.

(mm. 5–8):
(1.) You chased the gin - ger cat
(2.) Crash went the o - ran - ges } while Mum was in the loo!
(3.) Crash went the pile of plates } (*and Mum____ ne - ver knew.)
(4.) 'Got you!' said the mar - ket man

(mm. 9–12): (1–4.) Oh dear! Flop-py, what a naugh-ty thing to do.

(mm. 13–end):
You chased the gin - ger cat
Crash went the o - ran - ges
Crash went the pile of plates } and Mum ne - ver knew.
'Got you!' said the mar - ket man

*Alternative words!

The four verses fit pages 7, 9, 11, and 12.

Page 60

Stage 2 Wrens: The Headache

CD track 26: *All verses*

The Headache

Tune: Haydn Trumpet Concerto in E♭!

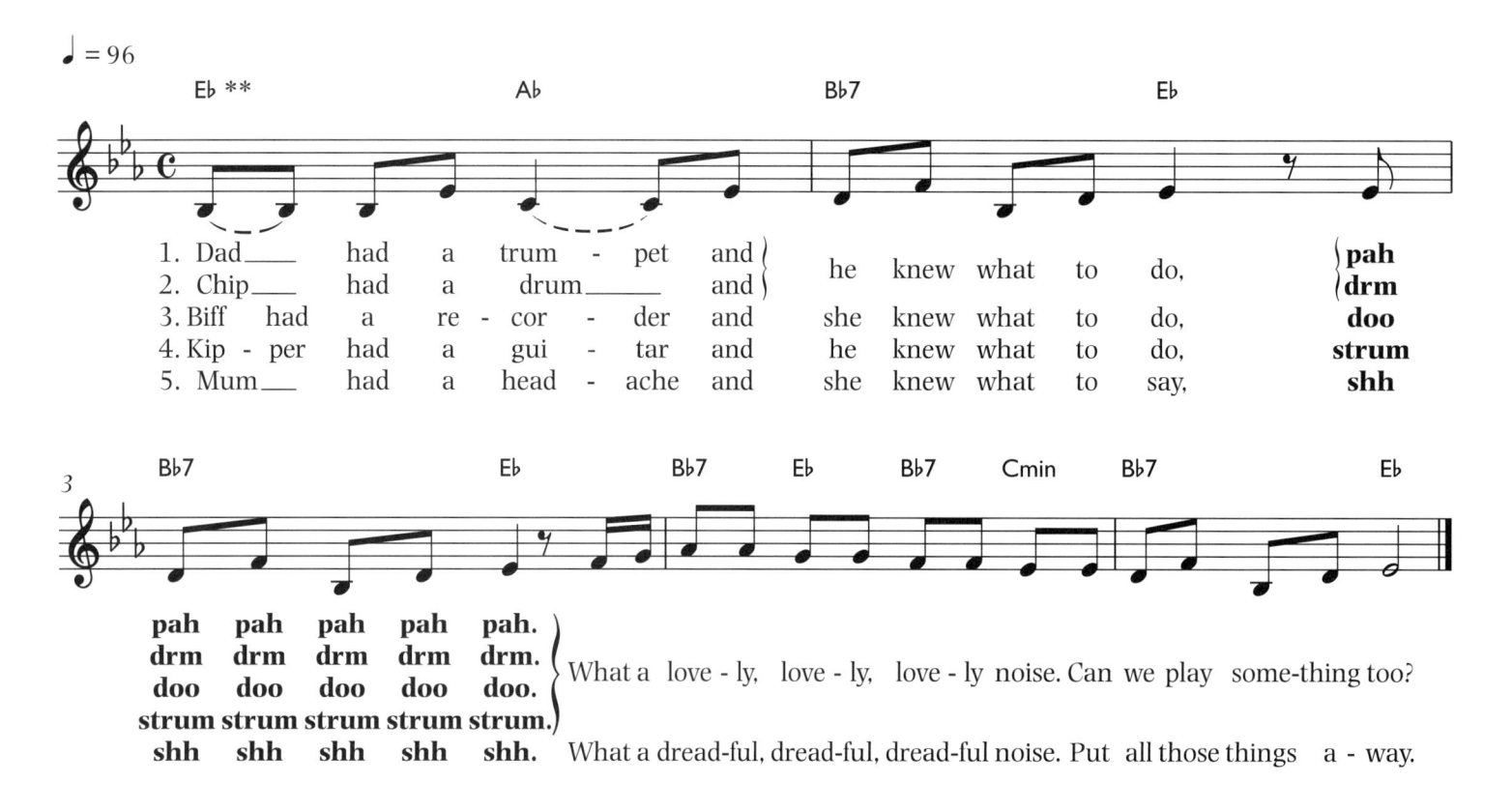

♩ = 96

1. Dad___ had a trum-pet and he knew what to do, **pah**
2. Chip___ had a drum___ and he knew what to do, **drm**
3. Biff had a re-cor-der and she knew what to do, **doo**
4. Kip-per had a gui-tar and he knew what to do, **strum**
5. Mum___ had a head-ache and she knew what to say, **shh**

pah pah pah pah pah.
drm drm drm drm drm.
doo doo doo doo doo.
strum strum strum strum strum. What a love-ly, love-ly, love-ly noise. Can we play some-thing too?
shh shh shh shh shh. What a dread-ful, dread-ful, dread-ful noise. Put all those things a-way.

Verse 1 fits page 1; verses 2 to 5 fit pages 2, 4, 6, and 7.

Play the rhythm of the words in **this type.**

** For capo chords see page 55.

36

At the Park

Tune: If you're happy and you know it

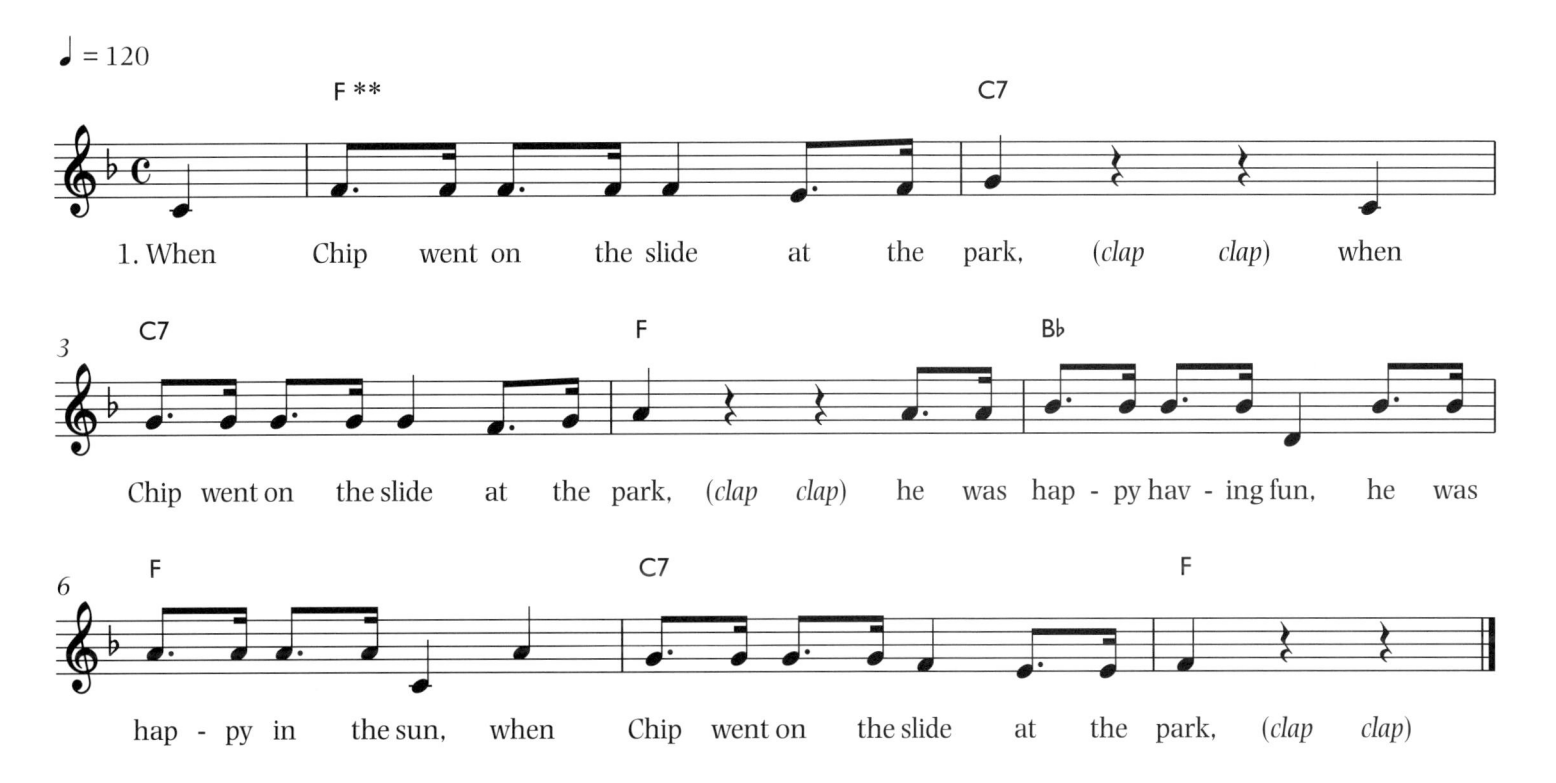

♩ = 120

1. When Chip went on the slide at the park, *(clap clap)* when Chip went on the slide at the park, *(clap clap)* he was hap-py hav-ing fun, he was hap-py in the sun, when Chip went on the slide at the park, *(clap clap)*

2. When Biff went on the horse . . . (*page 4*)

3. When Kipper went on the swing . . . (*page 6*)

4. When Mum went on the see-saw . . . (*page 7*)

5. When Floppy went to sleep . . . (*page 8*)

** For capo chords see page 55.

Stage 2 Wrens: Fancy Dress

CD track 28: *All verses*

Fancy Dress

Tune: Aiken Drum

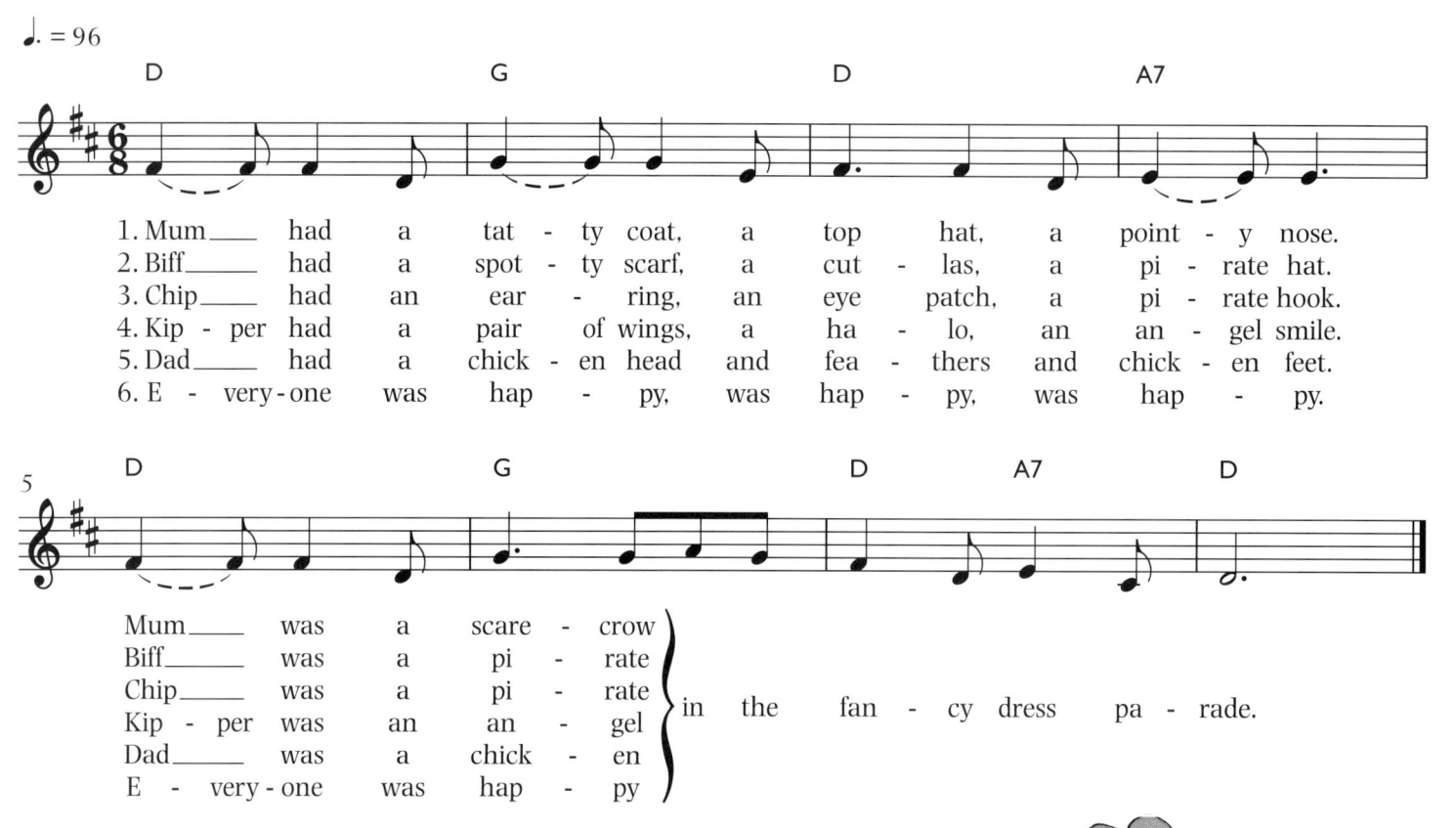

♩. = 96

1. Mum___ had a tat - ty coat, a top hat, a point - y nose.
2. Biff___ had a spot - ty scarf, a cut - las, a pi - rate hat.
3. Chip___ had an ear - ring, an eye patch, a pi - rate hook.
4. Kip - per had a pair of wings, a ha - lo, an an - gel smile.
5. Dad___ had a chick - en head and fea - thers and chick - en feet.
6. E - very - one was hap - py, was hap - py, was hap - py.

Mum___ was a scare - crow
Biff___ was a pi - rate
Chip___ was a pi - rate } in the fan - cy dress pa - rade.
Kip - per was an an - gel
Dad___ was a chick - en
E - very - one was hap - py

Verses 1 to 6 fit pages 1, 2, 3, 4, 6, and 8.

38

Push!

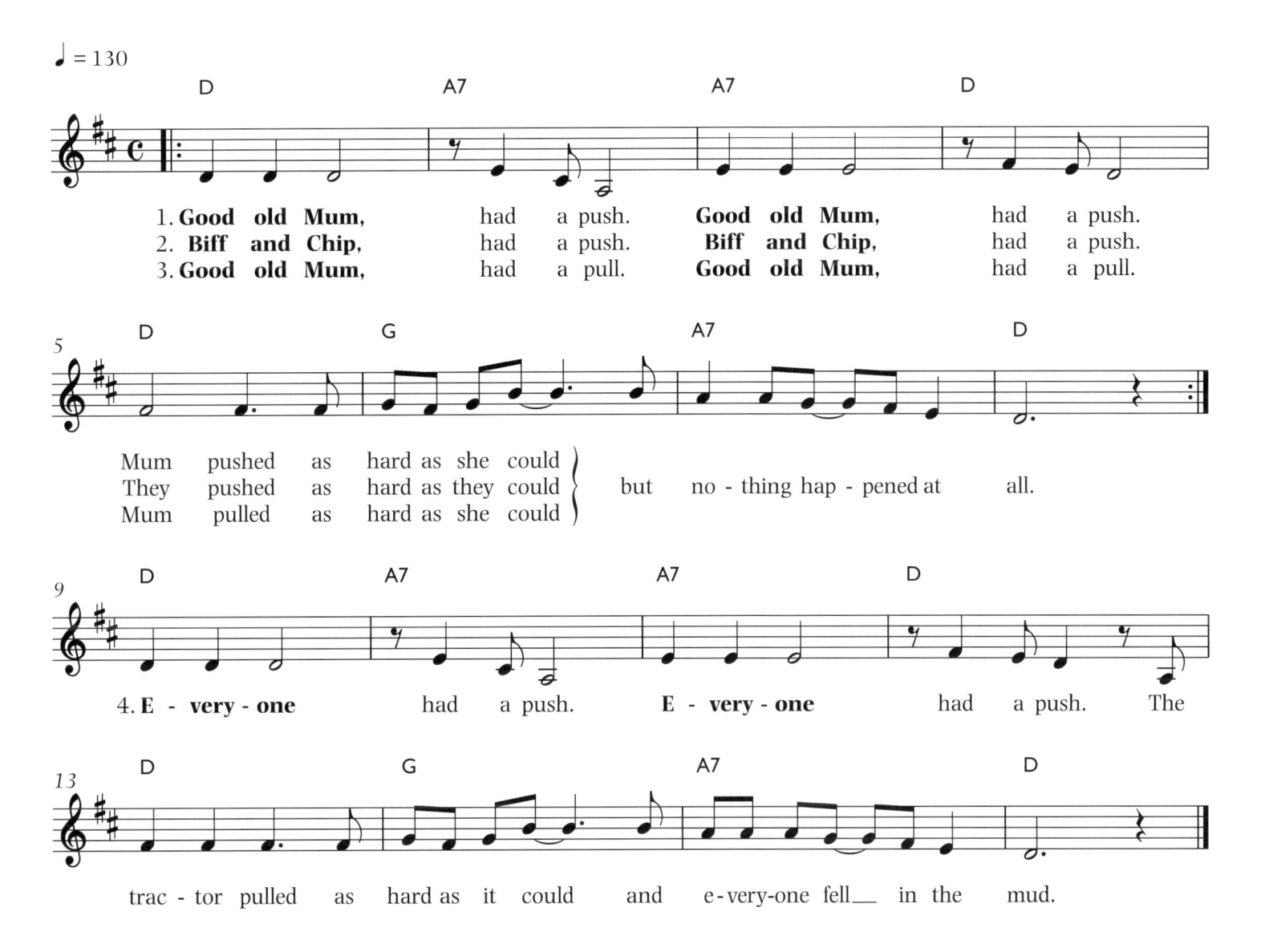

♩ = 130

1. **Good old Mum,** had a push. **Good old Mum,** had a push.
2. **Biff and Chip,** had a push. **Biff and Chip,** had a push.
3. **Good old Mum,** had a pull. **Good old Mum,** had a pull.

Mum pushed as hard as she could
They pushed as hard as they could } but no-thing hap-pened at all.
Mum pulled as hard as she could

4. **E-very-one** had a push. **E-very-one** had a push. The trac-tor pulled as hard as it could and e-very-one fell in the mud.

Verses 1 to 3 fit pages 2, 4, and 5; verse 4 fits pages 7 and 8.

Play the rhythm of the words in **this type.**

Page 61

Stage 2 Wrens: Good Old Mum   CD track 30: Verses 1, 3, 5, and 6

Good Old Mum

♩ = 110

*[Musical notation with chords: Eb**, Fmin, Bb7, Eb]*

1. **Good old Mum** put a big nose on. **Good old Mum** put a big nose on.

[Musical notation with chords: Eb, Ab, Bb7, Eb]

Good old Mum put a big nose on rea-dy for Christ-mas time.

Verse 1 fits page 1.

2. **Good old Mum** put a pillow on . . . (*page 2*)

3. **Good old Mum** put some big boots on . . . (*page 4*)

4. **Good old Mum** put big eyebrows on . . . (*page 6*)

5. **Good old Mum** put a big beard on . . . (*page 7*)

6. **Good old Mum** said 'Ho! Ho! Ho!' . . . (*page 8*)

> Play the rhythm of the words in **this type.**

** For capo chords see page 55.

Stage 2 Wrens: The Pet Shop CD track 31: *All verses*

The Pet Shop

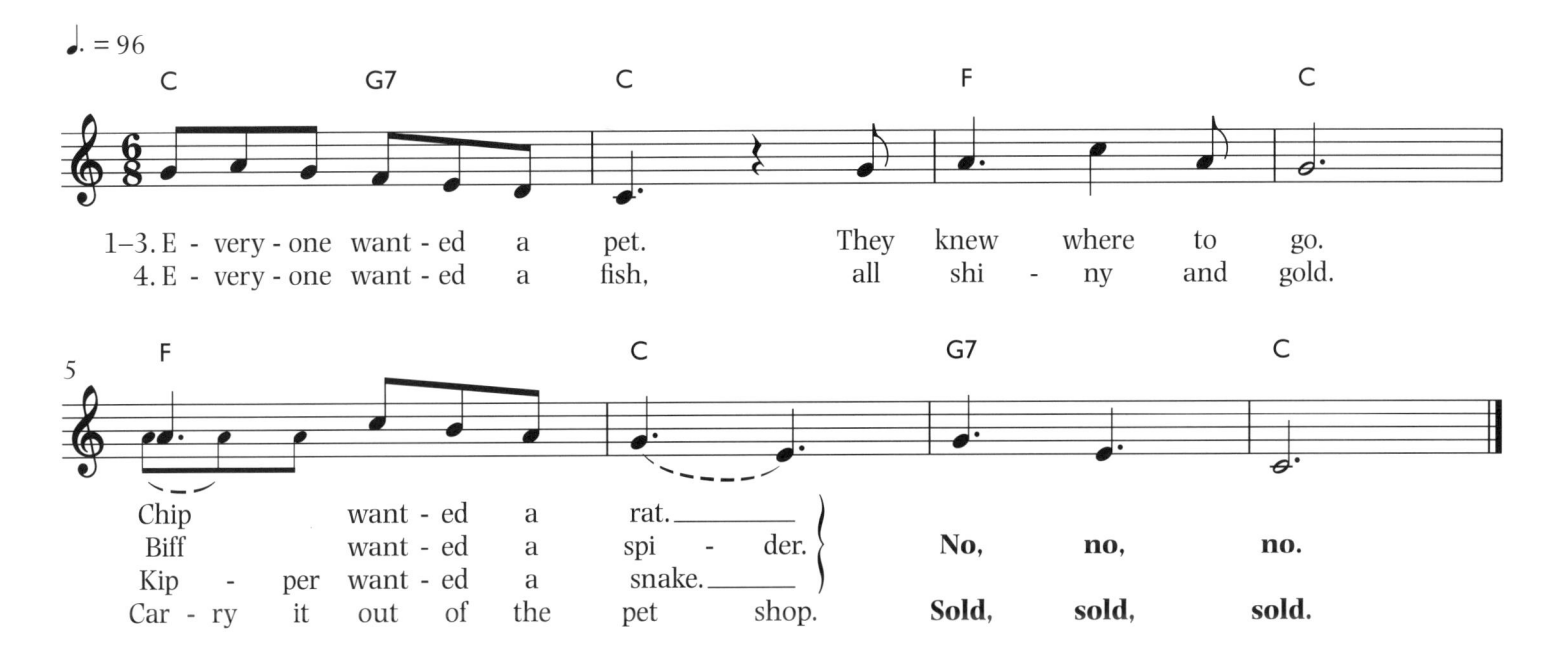

♩. = 96

1–3. E - very - one want - ed a pet. They knew where to go.
4. E - very - one want - ed a fish, all shi - ny and gold.

Chip want - ed a rat.
Biff want - ed a spi - der. **No, no, no.**
Kip - per want - ed a snake.
Car - ry it out of the pet shop. **Sold, sold, sold.**

Verse 1 fits pages 1 and 2; verses 2 to 4 fit pages 4, 6, and 8.

Play the rhythm of the words in **this type.**

41

Stage 2 More Wrens: What a Mess!   CD track 32: *All verses*

Everyone's Doing It

♩ = 104

VERSE

1–2. Everyone's doing it, doing it, doing it. Everyone's doing it, making a mess.

(1.) Look at Mum, she's making a dress.
(2.) Look at Dad, he's making some jam.
Everyone's making a mess.

CHORUS (after vv. 2, 4, and 5)

mess. So off we go to enter the show, and nobody will ever guess we're the best at making a mess.

Verse 1 fits page 1; verse 2 fits page 2.

3. (*page 4*)
   Everyone's doing it, doing it, doing it.
   Everyone's doing it, making a mess.
   Look at Chip, he's making a scarf.
   Everyone's making a mess. (*No chorus*)

4. (*page 5*)
   Everyone's doing it, doing it, doing it.
   Everyone's doing it, making a mess.
   Look at Biff, she's making a lorry.
   Everyone's making a mess.
   CHORUS: So off we go . . .

5. (*page 6*)
   Everyone's doing it, doing it, doing it.
   Everyone's doing it, making a mess.
   Look at Kipper, he's making a card.
   Everyone's making a mess.
   CHORUS: So off we go . . .

Page 64

** For capo chords see page 55.

Stage 2 More Wrens: Making Faces CD track 33: *All verses*

Making Faces

Tune: The muffin man

♩ = 72

| Eb ** | Eb | Fmin | F7 | Bb |

1. Dad can make a fierce — face, a fierce — face, a fierce — face.

| Eb | Eb | Ab | Bb | Eb |

Let's all make a fierce — face, one two three.

Verse 1 fits page 1.

2. Chip can make a sad face, . . . (*page 2*)

3. Biff can make a good face, . . . (*page 4*)

4. Mum can make a frightened face, . . . (*page 6*)

5. Kipper can make a hungry face, . . . (*page 8*)

** For capo chords see page 55.

Stage 2 More Wrens: The Journey   CD track 34: Verses 1, 4, and 5

The Journey

♩ = 120

1. We're going for a ride in the car to-day and we won't get *bored a-long the way. Not e-ven a lit-tle bit, per-haps just a lit-tle bit. Count to three with your eyes shut tight, **one two three.** Then e-very-thing will be quite all right, just you wait and see!

Verse 1 fits page 1.

For further verses, at * sing:

2. *hungry* (*page 2*)

3. *thirsty* (*page 3*)

4. *cross* (*page 4*)

5. *lost* (*page 6*)

Play the rhythm of the words in **this type.**

Page 61

Stage 2 More Wrens: Goal!   CD track 35: *All verses*

It's No Fun!

♩ = 82

1. *We're out in the park and it's no fun.* *We're cold and we're wet and it's no fun.* We're sorry we came, we won't come a-gain. *We're out in the park and it's no fun.*

5. Now Dad's scored a goal and it's great fun. Now Dad's scored a goal and it's great fun. We're happy we came, we'll all come a-gain. Now Dad's scored a goal and it's great fun.

Verse 1 fits pages 1 to 3; verse 5 fits page 8.

Replace the words in *italics* with:

2. Now *Floppy is tired* and it's no fun. (*page 4*)
3. Now *Kipper is *miserable* and it's no fun. (*page 5*)
4. Now *Mum is cross* and it's no fun. (*page 6*)

*If *miserable* is awkward, try *sad*.

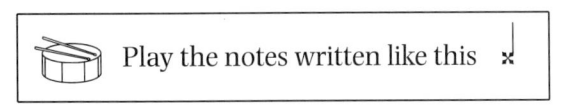

Play the notes written like this ✗

Stage 2 More Wrens: Who Did That? CD track 36: *All verses*

We're All Telling Tales

Tune: The farmer's in his den

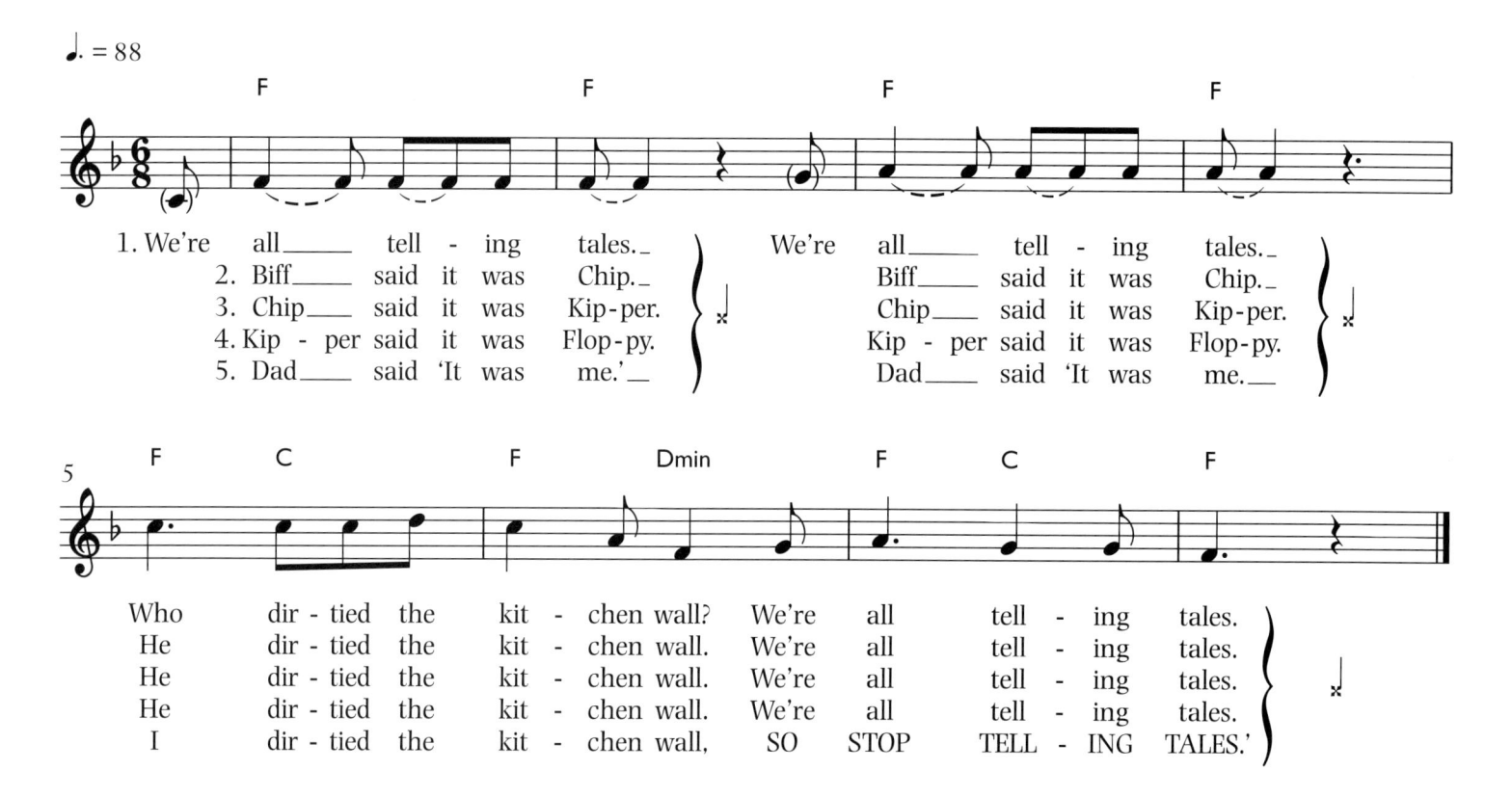

♩. = 88

1. We're all tell - ing tales. We're all tell - ing tales.
2. Biff said it was Chip. Biff said it was Chip.
3. Chip said it was Kip - per. Chip said it was Kip - per.
4. Kip - per said it was Flop - py. Kip - per said it was Flop - py.
5. Dad said 'It was me.' Dad said 'It was me.'

Who dir - tied the kit - chen wall? We're all tell - ing tales.
He dir - tied the kit - chen wall. We're all tell - ing tales.
He dir - tied the kit - chen wall. We're all tell - ing tales.
He dir - tied the kit - chen wall. We're all tell - ing tales.
I dir - tied the kit - chen wall, SO STOP TELL - ING TALES.'

Verses 2 to 5 fit pages 3, 4, 5, and 8.

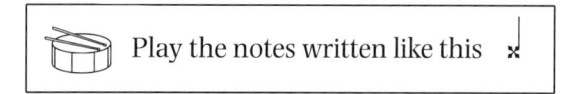

Play the notes written like this

46

Stage 2 More Wrens: Shopping — CD track 37: All verses

Sugar Calypso

♩ = 68

1. There was sugar in the supermarket, sugar in the shop. There was sugar on the market stall. Chip got crisps and a comic and a ball, but he never got sugar at all. There was white sugar on the shelf* but he never got sugar at all.

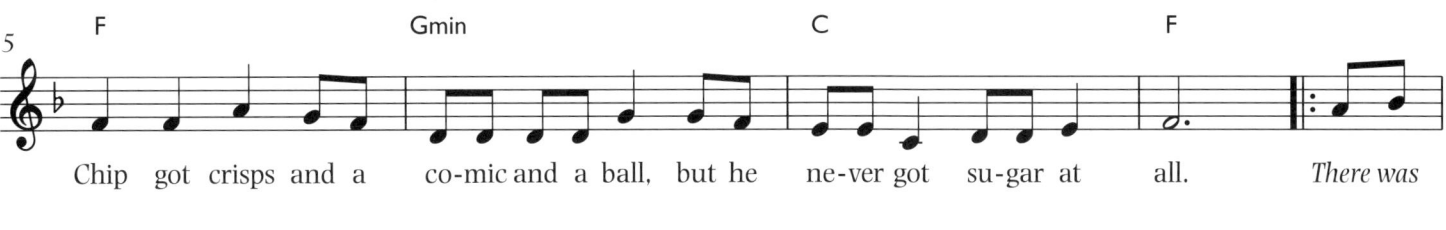

For verses 2 to 4, at * add an extra line for each verse, repeating the music of the *italic* section.

2. There was white sugar on the shelf,
   there was brown sugar on the shelf,
   but he never got sugar at all.

3. There was white sugar on the shelf,
   there was brown sugar on the shelf,
   there was icing sugar on the shelf, but he ...

4. ... *there were sugar cubes* ...

Let the children try saying the rhythm of these packets. You could make flash cards based on these packets for the children to chant.

Page 62

** For capo chords see page 55.

Stage 3 Wrens: Monkey Tricks CD track 38: Verses 1 and 5

At the Zoo

Tune: Here we go round the mulberry bush

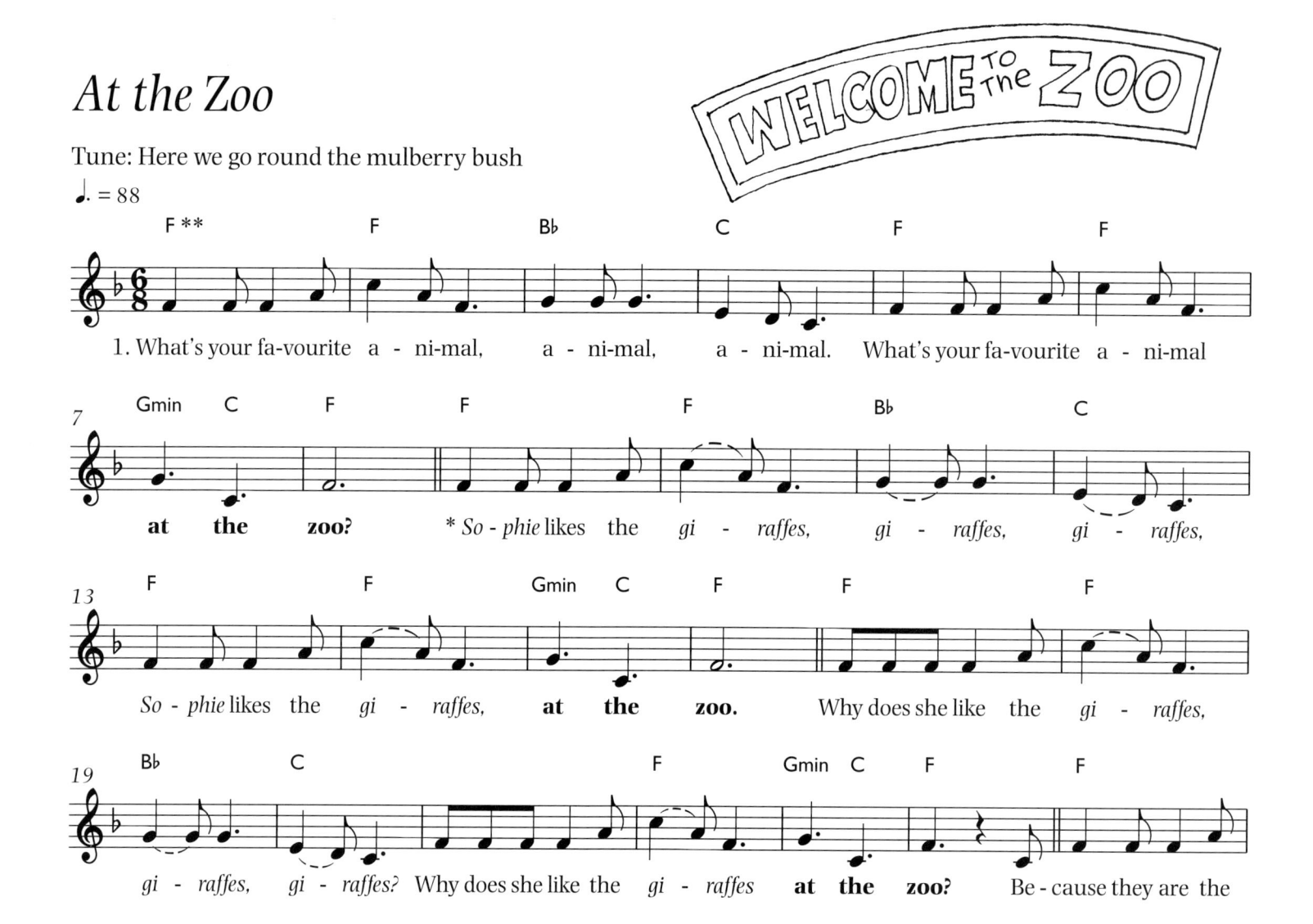

♩. = 88

1. What's your fa-vourite a-ni-mal, a-ni-mal, a-ni-mal. What's your fa-vourite a-ni-mal at the zoo? *So-phie likes the gi-raffes, gi-raffes, gi-raffes, So-phie likes the gi-raffes, **at the zoo.** Why does she like the gi-raffes, gi-raffes, gi-raffes? Why does she like the gi-raffes **at the zoo?** Be-cause they are the **tall— ones, tall— ones, tall— ones.** Be-cause they are the **tall— ones, at the zoo.**

Verse 1 fits page 3.

* Choose a different child for each verse. The child chooses the animal, from the book, and everybody sings about it. Replace the *italic* animal and adjective with the following:

2. ...seals...hungry (*page 5*)

3. ...crocodiles...sleepy (*page 7*)

4. ...parrots...noisy (*page 9*)

5. ...elephants...big (*page 11*)

6. ...monkeys...funny (*page 13*)

Or let them choose their own animal.

Play the rhythm of the words in **this type.**

** For capo chords see page 55.

48

Hey Presto!

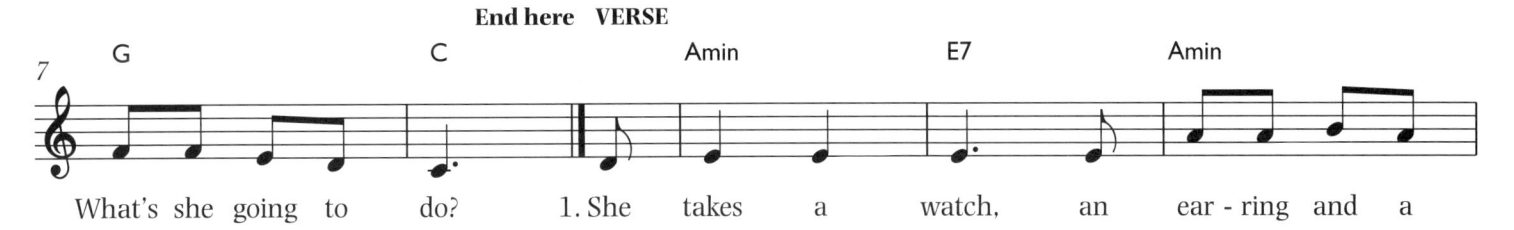

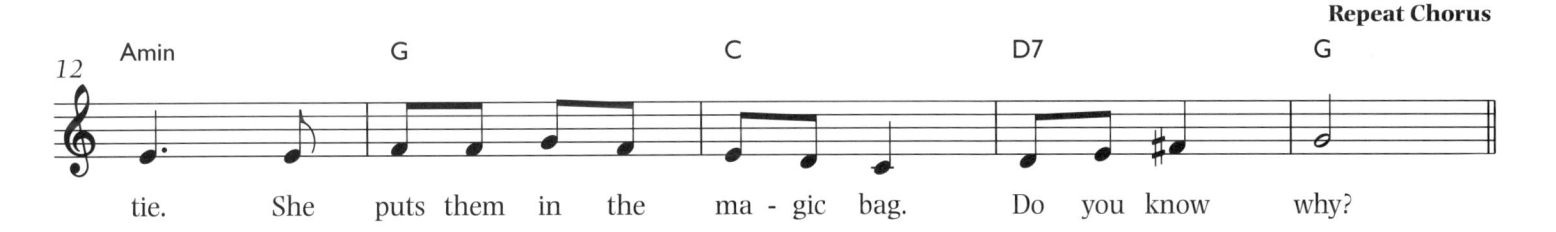

♩ = 112

CHORUS

Hey pres-to! Shee-na's got a trick for you. Hey pres-to!

End here VERSE

What's she going to do? 1. She takes a watch, an ear-ring and a

Repeat Chorus

tie. She puts them in the ma-gic bag. Do you know why?

Verse 1 fits pages 4 to 9.

2. She takes the bag, it's up on Dad's head now.
   She must be going to do a trick.
   Do you know how? (*page 10*)
   CHORUS: **Hey presto!** . . .

3. She's got a box, it's white and green and blue.
   And someone goes inside the box.
   Do you know who? (*page 12*)
   CHORUS: **Hey presto!** . . .

4. She takes her wand, she waves it in the air.
   And there's the earring, watch and tie.
   Do you know where? (*pages 14 to 16*)
   CHORUS: **Hey presto!** . . .

Play the rhythm of the words in **this type.**

Page 63

Stage 3 Wrens: It's the Weather

CD track 40: Verses 1, 2, 6, and 8

It's the Weather

♩. = 88

1. The wind was blow-ing through the town. The au-tumn leaves were fall-ing down. Then it start-ed to rain and the child-ren *were noi-sy a - gain. 'Oh dear!' said Mr - s May. 'Is-n't it hor-ri-ble wea-ther to-day, hor-ri-ble wea-ther to - day?'

8. The sun was shin-ing on the town. The sun was shin-ing all a-round. The hor-ri-ble wea-ther had passed and the chil-dren were good at last. 'What a day!' said Mr - s May. 'Is-n't it beau-ti-ful wea-ther to - day, beau-ti-ful wea-ther to - day?'

Verse 1 fits page 1.

At * sing:

2. *were silly* (*page 2*)
3. *were messy* (*page 4*)
4. *were untidy* (*page 5*)
5. *were cross* (*page 8*)
6. *were grumpy* (*page 9*)
7. *were unhappy* (*page 11*)

then sing verse 8 (*pages 14 to 15*)

Page 62

** For capo chords see page 55.

Stage 3 Wrens: A Sinking Feeling

CD track 41: *All verses*

The Orange Duck

♩ = 112

1. There's one person on the orange duck, orange duck, orange duck. There's one person on the orange duck. (*clap clap clap*) It's Wilma.

2. There are *two people on the orange duck, orange duck, orange duck. There are *two people on the orange duck. (*clap clap clap*) It's Wilma and Wilf.**

6. We've all fallen off the orange duck, orange duck, orange duck. We've all fallen off the orange duck. (*clap clap clap*) Oh no!

Verses 1 and 2 fit pages 2 and 5; verse 6 fits page 16.

At * change the number of people, and at ** add in the extra person's name, like this:

3. (*page 7*)
   * three
   (Wilma and Wilf) ** and Chip.

4. (*page 9*)
   * four
   (Wilma and Wilf) ** and Chip and Biff.

5. (*page 15*)
   * five
   (Wilma and Wilf) ** and Chip and Biff and Kipper.

Stage 3 Wrens: Naughty Children

CD track 42: *All verses*

A Safe Place

♩. = 112

1. If you want to climb
2. If you want to jump } find a safe place. (*clap clap*)
3. Play-ing with a ball

If you want to climb
If you want to jump } find a safe place. (*clap clap*)
Play-ing with a ball

If you want to climb
If you want to jump } find a safe place. (*clap*) Then
Play-ing with a ball

e-very-one (*clap*) can have some fun. (*clap*) Then

e-very-one can have some fun. (*clap clap*)

Page 63

Stage 3 Wrens: Creepy-crawly   CD track 43: *All verses*

Creepy-crawly

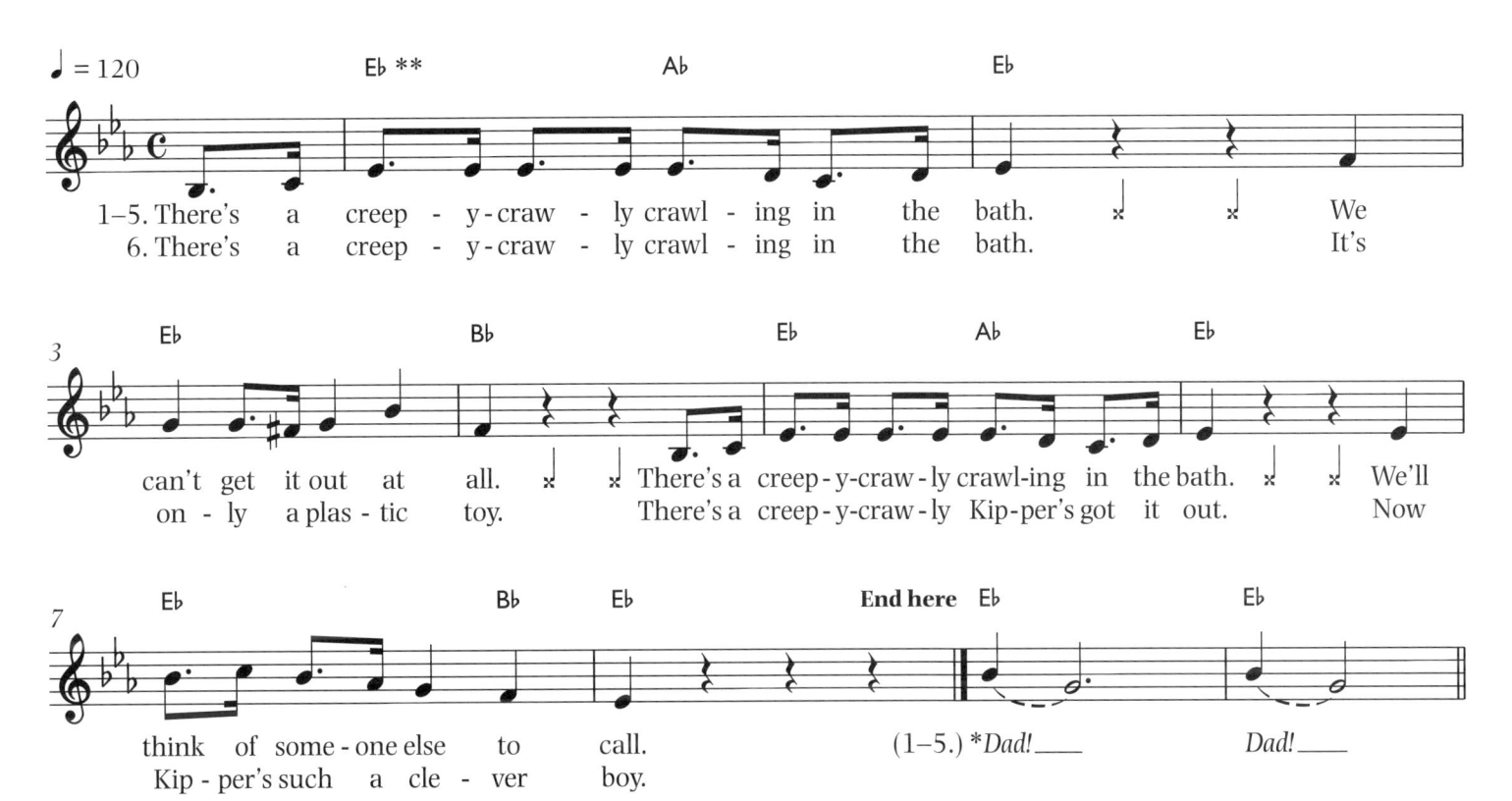

♩ = 120

1–5. There's a creep-y-craw-ly crawl-ing in the bath. We
6. There's a creep-y-craw-ly crawl-ing in the bath. It's

can't get it out at all. There's a creep-y-craw-ly crawl-ing in the bath. We'll
on-ly a plas-tic toy. There's a creep-y-craw-ly Kip-per's got it out. Now

think of some-one else to call. (1–5.) *Dad!___ Dad!___
Kip-per's such a cle-ver boy.

End here

Verse 1 fits pages 1 to 4.

At * call the next person:

2. *Mum! Mum!* (*page 5*)

3. *Chip! Chip!* (*page 8*)

4. *Biff! Biff!* (*page 11*)

5. *Kipper! Kipper!* (*page 15*)

Then sing verse 6 (*page 16*)

Play the notes written like this 𝄽

** For capo chords see page 55.

Guitar Chords

Example

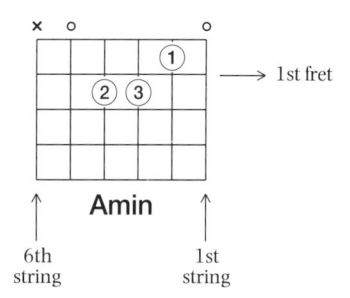

Amin

6th string → 1st string

1st fret →

The vertical lines represent the strings
The horizontal lines represent the frets
(a numeral to the left indicates the fret number)
A circle with a number inside shows where a finger
is to be pressed, and which finger is to be used
× indicates that a string is not to be played
o indicates that the string is open

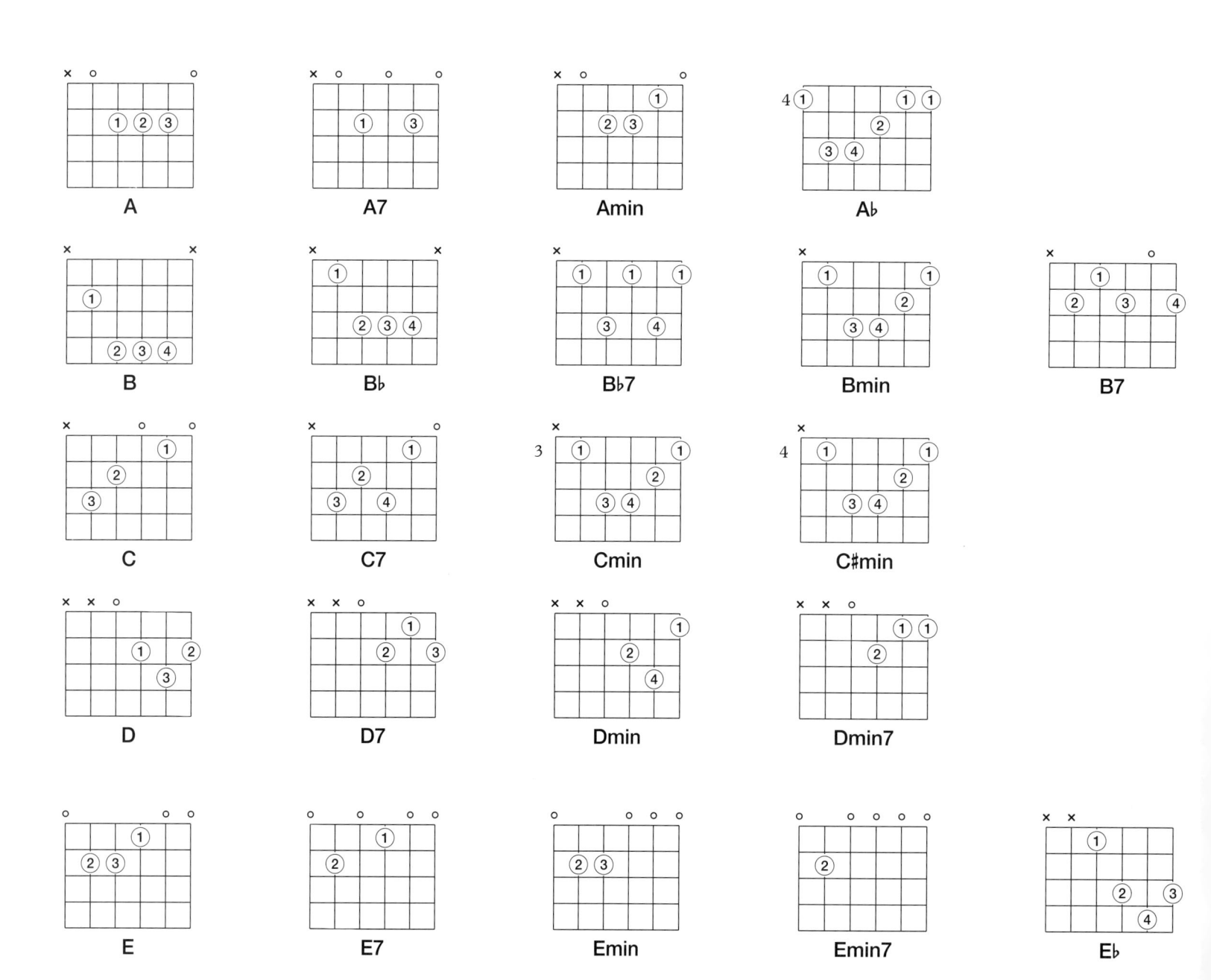

| A | A7 | Amin | A♭ |

| B | B♭ | B♭7 | Bmin | B7 |

| C | C7 | Cmin | C#min |

| D | D7 | Dmin | Dmin7 |

| E | E7 | Emin | Emin7 | E♭ |

54

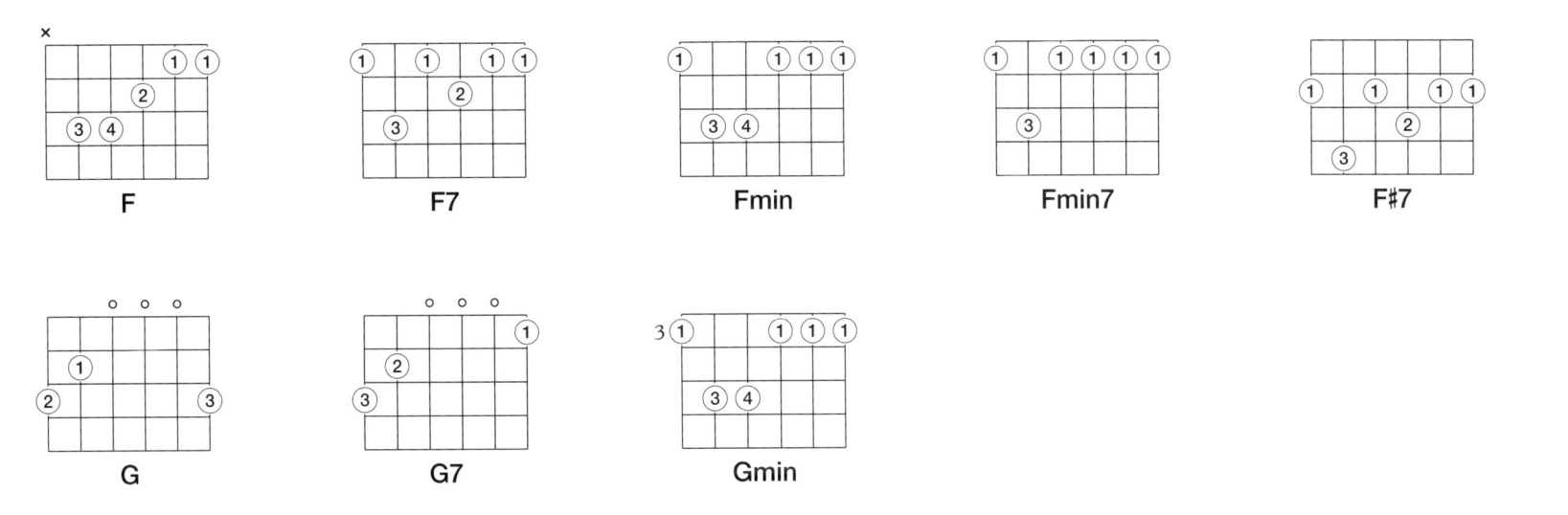

It's easier to use a capo for these songs. You could pencil in the alternative chords on the song page.

Title	Page	Capo	For	Play	For	Play	For	Play	For	Play	For	Play	For	Play	For	Play
A New Dog	20	1	Eb	D	Bb7	A7	Cm	Bm	Fm7	Em						
Floppy's Bath	24	1	Eb	D	Ab	G	Bb	A	Cm	Bm	Fm	Em				
Spots!	28	3	Cm	Am	Eb	C	Fm	Dm	G7	E7	D7	B7	C	A	Dm	Bm
Kipper's Laces	30	3	F	D	Gm	Em	C7	A7	Dm	Bm	C	A	G	E		
The Foggy Day	32	3	Cm	Am	Fm	Dm	G7	E7	C	A	F	D	G7	E7		
The Headache	36	1	Eb	D	Ab	G	Bb7	A7	Cm	Bm						
At the Park	37	3	F	D	C7	A7	Bb	G								
Good Old Mum	40	1	Eb	D	Fm	Em	Bb7	A7	Cm	Bm	Ab	G				
Everyone's Doing It	42	3	F	D	Gm	Em	C	A7	Bb	G						
Making Faces	43	1	Eb	D	Fm	Em	F7	E7	Bb	A	Ab	G				
Sugar Calypso	47	3	F	D	Gm	Em	C	A7								
At the Zoo	48	3	F	D	Bb	G	C	A7	Gm	Em						
It's the Weather	50	3	F	D	C	A7	Gm	Em	C7	A7						
Creepy-crawly	53	1	Eb	D	Ab	G	Bb	A								

Piano Accompaniments

These may be photocopied and enlarged as required. Bar numbers match those given on the song pages, and hence introductory bars are not counted.

New Trainers (page 19)

I've got (clap) new train-ers, (clap) I'll wear them (clap) when I go out to-day. I've got (clap) new train-ers, (clap) I'll wear them (clap) when I go out to play.

End here

VERSE

1. There's just one thing I must-n't for-get,_ they must-n't get dir-ty,_ they must-n't get wet. (three more verses)

Repeat Chorus

The Dreadful Dragon (page 23)

1. There once was a dread-ful dra-gon, it came to Biff one night with ter-ri-ble teeth and_ cru-el claws it was look-ing for a fight. Poor old Biff, what a hor-ri-ble dream, it gave you a nas-ty fright. Give your-self a shake! Now you're wide a-wake! E-very-thing's quite all right. (two more verses)

56

Let's Take Turns (page 22)

♩ = 120

Let's take turns, (let's take turns). Me and you, (me and you). Let's take turns, (let's take turns). E-very-thing we do, (e-very-thing we do). Play-ing a game, (play-ing a game). Hav-ing a ride, (hav-ing a ride). We'll have fun, (we'll have fun). Side by side, (side by side). Let's take turns, (let's take turns). E-very-day, (e-very-day). Let's take turns, (let's take turns). E-very time we play, (e-very time we play). Let's take turns, (let's take turns). Then join to-ge-ther to say, 'We're going to have fun be-cause we know the way'.

Spots! (page 28)

♩ = 110

1. I woke up to-day, I was-n't feel-ing right. I looked in the mir-ror, what a sight! I've got spots *(clap clap)* on my tum-my and my toes. Spots *(clap clap)* on my knees and my nose. Spots *(clap clap)* on my cheeks and my chin. What a spot-ty state I'm in! *(four more verses)*

** For capo chords see page 55.

Kipper's Laces (page 30)

♩ = 120

Kip-per's la-ces went **wig-gle wig-gle wig-gle.** Kip-per's la-ces went **jig-gle jig-gle jig-gle.** Kip-per's la-ces went **squig-gle squig-gle squig-gle.** Kip-per could-n't tie them yet. Kip-per was up-set. So he tried and tried, and tried and tried, and tried and tried all day. So he tried and tried, and tried and tried, then he did it. Hoo-ray!

** For capo chords see page 55.

Tooth Fairy (page 31)

Lyrics:
Tooth fairy, where are you? I've got something to say to you. Tooth fairy, bring the money and take my tooth away. Twenty P, fifty P. How much will you pay? Tooth fairy, bring the money and take my tooth away.

The Foggy Day (page 32)

Lyrics:
1–5. It's so foggy. We can't see. Dad's driven the car up onto the grass. We'll never get home for tea.

LAST VERSE

6. Don't be silly. It's O.K. Now Floppy and Mum are saying 'Hello!'. We'll get our tea today.

** For capo chords see page 55.

Floppy the Hero (page 34)

♩ = 140

1. Fire! Fire! Something's burning. Fire! Fire! Run with me. Nee-nah nee-nah, here's the en-gine. Come to the barn and see. *(three more verses)*

Mum Never Knew (page 35)

♩. = 88

1. Oh dear! Flop-py, what a naugh-ty thing to do. You chased the gin-ger cat while (*and Mum was in the loo! / Mum never knew.) Oh dear! Flop-py, what a naugh-ty thing to do. You chased the gin-ger cat and Mum ne-ver knew. *(three more verses)*

* Alternative words!

Push! (page 39)

♩ = 130

1. Good old Mum, had a push. Good old Mum, had a push. Mum pushed as hard as she could but nothing happened at all. *(four verses in all)*

4. Everyone had a push. Everyone had a push. The tractor pulled as hard as it could and everyone fell in the mud.

The Journey (page 44)

♩ = 120

1. We're going for a ride in the car today and we won't get bored along the way. Not even a little bit, perhaps just a little bit. Count to three with your eyes shut tight, **one two three.** Then everything will be quite all right, just you wait and see! *(four more verses)*

Sugar Calypso (page 47)

1. There was sugar in the supermarket, sugar in the shop. There was sugar on the market stall. Chip got crisps and a comic and a ball, but he never got sugar at all.

There was white sugar on the shelf* but he never got sugar at all.

(three more verses)

* v. 1: no repeat; v. 2: play twice; v. 3: play three times; v. 4: play four times.
** For capo chords see page 55.

It's the Weather (page 50)

1. The wind was blowing through the town. The autumn leaves were falling down. Then it started to rain and the children were noisy again. 'Oh dear!' said Mrs May. 'Isn't it horrible weather today, horrible weather today?'

(seven more verses)

** For capo chords see page 55.

62

Hey Presto! (page 49)

Everyone's Doing It (page 42)

♩ = 104

VERSE

1. E-veryone's doing it, doing it, doing it. E-veryone's doing it, making a mess. Look at Mum, she's making a dress. E-veryone's making a mess.

[vv. 1, 3.]

[vv. 2, 4, 5.] **CHORUS**

mess. So off we go to enter the show, and nobody will ever guess we're the best at making a mess.

[to vv. 3, 5.] [v. 5.]

** For capo chords see page 55.